BURPEE AMERICAN GARDENING SERIES

FLOWERING SHRUBS

BURPEE

AMERICAN GARDENING SERIES

FLOWERING SHRUBS

Ken Druse

PRENTICE HALL GARDENING

New York ◆ *London* ◆ *Toronto* ◆ *Sydney* ◆ *Tokyo* ◆ *Singapore*

This book is dedicated to Suzanne Frutig Bales who believes that
nothing is impossible.

PRENTICE HALL GENERAL REFERENCE
15 Columbus Circle
New York, NY 10023

PRENTICE HALL and colophon are registered trademarks
of Simon & Schuster Inc.

BURPEE is a registered trademark of W. Atlee Burpee & Company.

Library of Congress Cataloging-in-Publication Data

Druse, Ken.
    The Burpee American gardening series. Flowering shrubs / Ken
Druse.
        p.   cm.
    Includes index.
    ISBN 0-13-093717-7
    1. Flowering shrubs.   2. Flowering shrubs—Pictorial works.
I. Title.   II. Title: Flowering shrubs.
SB435.D78   1992
635.9'76—dc20   91-15734
                                                  CIP

Designed by Patricia Fabricant and Levavi & Levavi
Manufactured in the United States of America

10   9   8   7   6   5   4   3   2   1

First Edition

Cover: *Ruth and Jim Levitan's magnificent garden in spring features flowering trees, woodland
wildflowers, all manner of bulbs and the heart of the garden, flowering shrubs.*

Preceding pages: *Colorful flowering shrubs form the backbone of your garden. Blooming in turn, they
are the inhabitants of the human-scale layer—the place where your eye naturally comes to rest.*

CONTENTS

Introduction

Trees tower above the landscape. Annuals and herbaceous perennials come and go. But shrubs form the lasting framework for our garden designs. These plants are the flesh and bones of the landscape, the place to hang our flower plantings or drape our clambering vines. They are truly four-season plants; in spring, many flower. Foliage contributes through the year for some. Tracery twigs and branches catch the snow, making sculptural forms in the winter landscape. In sunshine or shade, shrubs are the most useful plants for our homesites.

Shrubs are woody plants that do not die back like the herbaceous, nonwoody perennials. They are smaller than trees, of course, and when they reach their height at maturity, they do not continue to add new wood to grow taller. They just become thicker, more dense and replace aging and dead growth with fresh twigs.

If the shrub has a single main trunk, like the trees, it usually breaks into branches rather close to the base. This is what creates the distinction between a large shrub, like a serviceberry, and a flowering dogwood tree of the same height. Some of these shrubs will reach a certain size and will grow no taller. They may die—shrubs don't live as long as trees—but more often, these plants will send up another shoot or two to take the place of the original, central trunk. Many other shrubs produce new shoots annually that come up from the ground, like the Japanese kerria, whose new canes emerge from a subterranean root stock to form a clump, just as bamboo and herbaceous peonies do. It could be said that a shrub has bushy growth, but generally the word *bush* is used in conjunction with a type of plant, such as a rose bush or a blueberry bush. *Shrub* is the word we will use here.

Bush sounds a bit like "blob." Our elegant shrubs are so much more. They are individuals. Learning to treat a plant as unique and singular is one of the most important steps toward becoming a successful gardener. It's more thoughtful not to lump them as so many people do, "We need some bushes for the backyard." Or worse, the archaic notion that bushes must be placed completely around the perimeter of a house—to anchor it—as if without them, the house would fly off into the stratosphere. It reminds me of the landscape architect's affinity for the term *plant material*. That brings the shrubs down to the lowest position possible: equal to a clay brick, lump of gravel or asphalt. What does that say about the fragrant Korean spicebush, or the exalted majesty of a fountain of weigela, the romance of the fragrant lilac or the regal presence of the mature rhododendron?

The shrubs are alive. They have some of the ephemeral, fleeting transience of life itself. Some of their branches do die, but many last for years. New growth is added to the general shape and volume of the mature shrub. But once it has reached its ultimate size, the system of gain and loss is checked and balanced to maintain the ultimate mass. Shrubs are so important to us because they are of human scale. They are the plants at eye level, and perhaps we make a subconscious connection. We do not revere or bow down to them like the stately trees. We don't find them precious like the early spring bulbs' flowers. These plants are our equals. We meet, nod, acknowledge our shared space on earth and go on our way. The shrubs live long, compared to most perennials and certainly to the annuals, but they don't live as long as most trees; we have that in common with them, too.

When your shrubs have reached maturity and explode with blossoms in their season, you can sigh and take pride in the accomplishment. In our gardens, we share the credit; especially if we have perfectly chosen and sited the plant and helped it grow strong—nursing it in harsh times, basking in its reflected glory in good times, nurturing it always. We can glory in the healthy, happy, well-adjusted shrub. It is a reflection of our success as good "parents," caretakers of one of nature's miraculous inventions. These may be the most important plants in our home landscapes. Every other element, lawn trees, patio and path, swirl around the human-scaled flowering shrubs—the plants that remind us of our place in nature.

A meandering grass path flows through plantings of spring-blooming evergreen and deciduous azaleas under dogwood trees. This garden also uses the bare twigs of pruned rose of Sharon to great effect.

THE FLOWERING SHRUB PLANNER

NATURE'S HAND

Nature abhors a vacuum. Open land if left, even for a little while, begins to change. First the opportunistic plants, what we might call weeds or maybe wildflowers and meadow grasses, take hold. In a year or so, woody plants brought to this place as seeds by birds or borne on the wind, sprout. These are the shrubs and trees.

These seedlings continue to grow, and in a few more years, the open land is covered with good-size shrubs and small trees. In time, the trees grow up and shade out much of the underplantings. Some shade-tolerant shrubs exist in the shadows cast by the taller trees. Along the edge of open land or by rivers, lakes and streams, the shrubs of the understory flourish in great variety. Some hydrangeas, sweet pepperbushes, rhododendron, mountain laurels and shrub dogwood grow there. In hot, dry climates or in places with poor, rocky soil, the trees may never get a good foothold, and the sun-loving, low woody shrubs remain. Rockroses, brooms and California lilacs are among those that continue to eke out an existence in this moisture- and nutrient-starved environment. These persistent plants, the flowering shrubs, are the progenitors of the ornamental shrubs for our home gardens.

USES OF SHRUBS IN THE LANDSCAPE

Not only does nature supply these shrubs, it also provides suggestions on how to use them in the landscape. Inspiration for informal shrub designs comes from this model. Under tall trees in a shady garden shrubs can be planted. Such shrubs as the oak-leafed hydrangea, Carolina allspice, fothergilla, redvein enkianthus and Virginia sweet spire populate middle-layer plantings above ferns and shade-loving wildflowers.

If you live by the edge of a wooded area, then the shrubs that populate those transitional areas, the ones that "introduce" the forest, would offer recommendations for you. Viburnums in variety, witch hazels and sweet bay magnolia could be included. If space allows, a nearly wild area could be developed for the outside boundaries of your property. A selection of trees to include some of those that live in the wild places around you as well as similar ones from other parts of the world could be garnered for your collection. In front of these, masses of shrubs would provide a transition from the maintained areas of your yard, the lawn or flower plantings, to simulate the forest understory and add interest in a space too often left barren.

A deep screen could be developed for a large property by planting a variety of large shrubs that bloom in turn along the edge. Not only do these shrubs hide a view but they also dampen traffic noise and reduce the effects of wind—all while adding the visual interest of their forms

Just as shrubs in nature line the woodland edge, so too will they form a perfect transition from lawn to tall trees. The meeting of horizontal lawn to vertical trees is softened by this flowering shrub mediator.

The colorful coral blossoms of a deciduous azalea highlight the base of a city gardener's staircase. A decorative flower pot atop a classical column punctuates this formal statement.

and beautiful flowers. Shrubs can actually cool the environment by adding shade and reducing glare and reflected and radiant heat. Their leaves transpire, cooling the air with evaporating moisture. In a situation like this, a screen of shrubs that bloom sequentially, you could select from an enormous variety of shrubs. The only limitation would be that they all had similar requirements as to soil, light and moisture. Here in an informal screen, a shrub such as the mock orange would be welcome. It has the scale and form and leaf surface to do the job. But, because it blooms for a relatively short time and adds little in the way of foliage

color or texture, fall or winter interest, berries or fruit, it might not do for small gardens. There, we demand more from our shrubs —they have to perform during at least two seasons, or bloom for several weeks.

Out-of-the-way places present chances to use some wonderful specimens that may or may not offer long-season color. These are occasionally viewed spots where little else will grow, or waste areas where you want some color and texture, but you will not be able to supply extra water, or other maintenance needs. Perhaps along the roadside, behind the garage, in a low, moist spot, or among the rocks of a natural outcrop, such

plants as slender deutzia, Australian bottlebrush, buckeye and bush honeysuckle could fit the bill. Security hedges can be made from flowering shrubs, too. For places where meticulous, high-maintenance evergreen hedges or nonliving, chain-link fence might not be the best choices, flowering quince or, better still, the hardy trifoliate orange, with its razor-sharp thorns, could be more useful than barbed wire and infinitely more beautiful.

Many shrubs are also low groundcovers, and some can hold an embankment. These plants are perfect for "streetscapes" or steep slopes that tumble down to the road and climb up across the street. Even dwarf forsythia varieties such as *Forsythia × intermedia* 'Arnold Dwarf' could be pressed into service. Aaron's-beard St.-John's-wort with large, yellow flowers all summer long is a cover just greater than 1 foot tall. Vines can be allowed to climb up through the shrubs to add color from flowers when the shrubs themselves may not be in bloom. Clematis varieties would work well, as would variegated porcelain berry or magnolia vine with red berries that form even in the shade of dense shrubs. The prerequisite for selecting shrubs for the "out back" is that they be perfectly situated. Place moisture lovers in a wet area, sun lovers to bask in the solar rays, shade lovers in the shadows, drought-tolerant candidates in fast-draining sites. This is one of the keys to growing any plant successfully.

These suggestions for using

Formality is also enhanced by repeating two similar elements. These cerise Camellia japonica *shrubs flank the gateway to the formal rose garden at Filoli in northern California.*

flowering shrubs in informal settings don't exclude their use in the formal garden or formal spaces around your home. Usually the areas around the house and the utility places, walkways, access to outdoor meters and storage areas, for example, are paved to some degree. The flowering shrubs can be worked into schemes there as well. However, much care must be exercised as to selection. These shrubs should be chosen for long interest, even if that just means evergreen foliage. And they should also stay in bounds with as little pruning as possible. Small-leafed evergreen rhododendron, usually called "azaleas," can be used to good advantage next to brick paving and around the patio edge. The new 'Robin Hill' hybrids with enormous white or pink flowers in late spring and well into summer are alternatives to the familiar suburban magenta and hot orange spring kinds. These plants have flowers more like petunias than the minitrumpet-flowered Kurume azaleas. Glossy abelia could be another choice. It is semievergreen and blooms for months, from late spring often into fall, in sun or partial shade. The shiny bronze-green foliage is also useful. Pruning will be needed from time to time if they spread and become obstructive.

Repeating symmetrical elements always imparts an air of formality, whether that's with a pair of urns or twin daphnes flanking the steps to the front door. Rows of shrubs on either side of a front walk can also be elegant. Even large shrubs could

be used. Imagine rows of camellias in a shaded area on either side of a straight, or even a winding, path. These midsize shrubs bloom winter to spring, by variety, and have glossy evergreen leaves year 'round.

A flowering-shrub collection is the perfect foil for ornamental plantings. The traditional perennial border is nearly always backed by a wall or, more often, by a screen of shrubs. Flowering shrubs would do more than, say, a needle evergreen hedge—they would produce flowers that would contribute to the colorful effects through the season. A narrow access path, hidden behind the tallest plantings at the back of the border, could

separate the flower planting from the flowering-shrub tableau; it would give access to both the back of the herbaceous border and the front of the flowering-shrub planting—yet be invisible to visitors who see this planting from the front only.

Large shrubs can be used to define spaces in the garden or landscape. These "walls" create "rooms" for flower plantings, or better, to furnish with more flowering shrubs. Tall lilacs, viburnums, rose of Sharons or even pussy willows could make the framework. For the rooms' "interiors," one could assemble variegated *Daphne × Burkwoodii* 'Carol Mackie', purple smoke bush or *Kerria*

A single flowering shrub in the lawn can in itself be an arresting formal element. Isolated a bit from the crowd, this spike winter hazel has a grand and elegant presence.

Big-leafed hydrangeas and mature evergreens gracefully direct visitors to an elegant stairway. A sudden level change becomes an opportunity to create a garden masterpiece.

The complementary colors of common lilac and creamy yellow 'Lady Bank's' rose create a spectacular spring picture which, however fleeting, makes an unforgettable memory and a lasting impression on the landscape.

Flowering shrubs can be beautiful landscape problem-solvers, too. This naturalized planting of assorted azaleas forms a river of color where grass lawn would be difficult to mow.

species along with a decorative iron bench or table and chairs.

A single, grand specimen in the lawns is perhaps the most effective living formal element. One terrific flowering shrub, perhaps a peegee hydrangea, bottlebrush buckeye, tree lilac or fringe tree, would make a spectacular addition to the front yard, even where space is limited. Just take precautions to keep lawn mowers and "weed wackers" away from the base of the shrubs. A simple solution is a circle of mulch around the base of the plants, or a more formal mowing strip. This is a line of paving, usually brick, designed for the mower wheel to ride on, that keeps the mower away from the plant's trunk.

The top of a masonry retaining wall might be the place for a cascading bridal wreath whose arching stems, covered in spring with white, buttonlike flower clusters, would soften the wall's hard architecture without destroying its formal presence. Shrubby cinquefoil would be the choice for a curbside in sun. Poolside plantings of larger evergreen rhododendron and hydrangeas can hide the fences that are required by law in most municipalities.

Shrubs can be used to direct traffic as well. Arranged shrubs can tell the meter reader which way to turn to find the object of his or her mission. A line of shrubs broken in the center can keep people from walking across the lawn and let them know from a distance where the entry path begins. Massed shrubs in corners can direct visitors while creating a spectacular display in an otherwise unused spot.

And a fragrant shrub should always be placed in an unavoidable spot. Imagine turning a corner in the path to come right up next to a lilac. A pink-flowered sweet pepperbush would be a good choice for a spot frequented in summer.

All of these shrubs represent more than the fleeting color of their flowers or the short-lived beauty of, say, annuals. These are permanent additions to the landscape. They may require an investment at first, but they will pay off in the long run by increasing your property value, and along the way they will continue to pay dividends in the form of lovely flowers, ornamental fruits, foliage textures, autumn colors and winter interest from bark and branches forming tracery patterns against the sky and sketching shadowy etchings in the snow.

A large planting bed of mixed shrubs, trees and herbaceous perennials is highlighted in spring by a flowering Fothergilla gardenii *(right). Soft fuzzy tufts grow from the tips of the branches in partial shade or sun (you might even try it in shade if there is bright light). Fabulous fall foliage color is a bonus of this handsome plant.*

Natural Shrub Shapes

The flowering shrubs, especially the deciduous ones, have wonderful natural shapes. They do not need to be pruned, except for the removal of dead wood. If they are well sited they will not outgrow their spaces to cover the walk or obscure a window. However, that is the case in a perfect world without inherited foundation plantings, or ice storms that split a shrub in two. When pruning, or planning, it is helpful to know something about the natural shapes of shrubs. You may have to restore the natural shape of a shrub that has, through some twist of environmental fate, gone off course.

Fastigiate, or columnar, shrubs are upright and slim—taller than they are wide. Rose of Sharon, sweet pepperbush and buckthorn are more upright than horizontal growing in general, but the true cylindrical shrubs are usually cultivars bred to maintain this shape.

Globe-shaped shrubs form controlled mounds that are very round and compact in their natural state. Evergreen azaleas and most rhododendron are globe shaped.

Vase-shaped shrubs have the form of feather dusters. They are gathered at the base and shoot up and out toward the sky. Weigela is an example.

Weeping shrubs are shaped like fountains, with many stems shooting up and cascading down like water droplets. Examples are bridal wreath (Spiraea × Vanhouttei) and larger forsythia varieties.

Spreading, or prostrate, are those low shrubs that can be used for the front of a planting or as groundcovers. Rockrose (Cistus species), Aaron's-beard St.-John's-wort (Hypericum calycinum) and shrubby cinquefoil (Potentilla fruticosa) are examples.

Rounded shrubs are shaped like trees but emanate from several trunks or from one trunk that branches at the base. See Magnolia species, fringe tree (Chionanthus virginicus) and peegee hydrangea for examples.

Rambling shrubs are taller than the low spreaders but they, too, flow in every direction. Japanese kerria (Kerria japonica), and blue mist spirea (Caryopteris species) are ramblers.

Colonizers spread to naturalize over an entire area. See false spirea Sorbaria sorbifolia.

Pyramidal, or conical, shrubs look like Christmas trees. These are needled evergreens, for the most part.

At California's Blake Gardens, Nandina domestica (center) blooms happily in USDA Zone 9. This elegant scene belies the tenacity of the tropical-looking "heavenly bamboo." Not a true bamboo, but undeniably celestial. This sturdy plant will grow well in USDA Zone 7, and with protection, in Zone 6. Flowers, fruit and fall foliage color are added enticements.

THE PLANTINGS

It is unusual to see a single shrub growing on its own in the wild, and when there are several shrubs, they are rarely of different species. To effect the most natural, or better, aesthetically pleasing creation include several of each shrub, just as you would have several of each perennial in a border. Then your schemes look more like drifts that interweave in the landscape.

The line of shrubs for a screen planting or at the edge of the property should include selections with varied texture, size and flower color, if this area is to be more than just a demarcation of the boundary. For example, on a smaller property, this kind of planting becomes a shrub border. It is planned and scaled just as if it were a herbaceous perennial border, only in this case, made up of woody, flowering shrubs. Evergreen shrubs should be included for winter interest, but also for their texture. That's especially the case with needled evergreens not known for their flowers.

Now you've learned a lot about the flowering shrubs and can't wait to apply this knowledge. But resist the temptation of choosing every glorious flowering shrub that money can buy. Pause and ponder. What can the flowering shrubs do for you and your property? The thoughtful, well-planned use of these exquisite plants is the mark of the truly artful landscape designers. Sharing nature's bounty and making one of its greatest gifts work for you is the test of your horticultural know-how.

DESIGNING WITH FLOWERING SHRUBS

SELECTION

Let's get specific. Is the shrub evergreen, semievergreen or deciduous? For the most part, evergreen shrubs are used for hedges and screens and for their solid forms in winter. The deciduous kinds are most often those grown for flowers, and they usually do have more and showier blossoms. Some shrubs are semievergreen. Glossy abelia loses some of its leaves in cold climates, nearly none in warm spots. Some other "evergreens" have leaves that last two years. They are constantly replacing the two-year-old leaves with new ones, but no one really notices this—the plant seems to always be clothed in green leaves. Small-leafed, evergreen rhododendron, the ones we call "azaleas," often have leaves that last one or two years. One set is produced in spring and another set is produced midseason. They last until new leaves push them off the plant, so the effect is the same as it would be if the plant were totally evergreen.

Deciduous shrubs lose their leaves every autumn and remain bare through the winter, just like the deciduous trees. Plan to include some that produce brilliant fall color such as fothergilla. Some of these deciduous shrubs may behave like herbaceous perennials in cold climates. Butterfly bush, for example, may die to the ground in severe winters and sprout new "woody" growth right from the hardy roots. Semiwoody shrubs such as butterfly bush and *Vitex* produce flower buds on new growth; otherwise the winter kill would result in a leafy plant with no blossoms at all. Late winter- and spring-blooming shrubs have flowers that sprout on the growth produced the previous growing season. For that reason, we don't prune them until just after flowering; otherwise we would be removing the flowering mechanisms for the following season. If we wait too long to prune, we might remove next year's developing flower buds.

Needled evergreen shrubs, such as pines, yews and junipers, are not what we're about here. We want to concentrate on the ornamental ones that bloom, and bloom quite a bit. Selecting shrubs for your landscape takes forethought. You have to decide what the purpose of the shrub will be, what conditions you have, what color flowers you want and when you want them and the other aesthetic effects, such as winter interest, foliage texture and possibly, fall color and fruit.

Selecting Shrubs

The considerations for selecting shrubs begin with knowledge of the conditions *in situ*. Climate is first and foremost. Can the shrub you want grow in your climate? You'll have a pretty good chance with shrubs bought at the local garden center, or better still, from a nearby grower. But I have seen shrubs offered at the nursery in flower that really could not be grown locally. A plant that is not damaged by frost is said to be *hardy*, one that cannot stand frost is *tender*. Hardiness refers to a plant's ability to withstand temperatures in your area. Shoppers often ask nursery personnel, "Is this plant hardy?" They may be asking about a tropical houseplant. And the answer is invariably yes. Hardy has come to mean tough and resilient.

Large-leafed evergreen rhododendron make a perfect background foil for this elegant sculpture —in and out of flower. Thoughtful siting is a mark of garden mastery.

A weeping bridal wreath *(Spiraea × Vanhouttei) chases a garden nymph through a colonized planting of flowering shrubs at Magnolia Plantations in Charleston, South Carolina.*

Winterthur's famous azaleas carpet the understory of the edited woodland where light filters through the tree-top canopy to provide the partial shade that suits them best.

What you want to know is whether the plant is frost hardy, able to withstand minimum temperatures in your area.

The U.S. Department of Agriculture has made a map of hardiness zones in the United States (pages 90–91). These tell us what the minimum temperature in any area is expected to be. Learn your zone number. For example, if you live in an area where the temperature generally goes down to between 0° and 10°F, then you live in Zone 7, and you know that most shrubs listed as appropriate for Zones 5 to 8 will do well in your area. The zone reference, unfortunately, does not consider heat. A plant that is happy in Zone 5 will certainly survive the Zone 7 winter, but the summer might prove too hot for it and, in some cases, too humid. You'll have to learn by observation and find a nursery person you can rely on, or call your Cooperative Extension Service agent, usually listed in the telephone book, for recommendations.

Plants listed for Zone 7 generally will survive in that zone, but there can be winters with exceptionally low temperatures as well as extenuating environmental circumstances, such as drought or flooding, that affect success. Your own property has pockets of warmth or cold, called "micro-climates." Cold air may pour down a hillside and pool in a low spot that can actually stay colder than the rest of your lot. A place against a south-facing wall can be much warmer than other parts of the property. Learn about your yard's micro-climates, and use them to your advantage. You might select a shrub that is especially hardy or late-spring blooming for the cold spot and grow a marginally hardy specimen in the warm place.

Locations near large bodies of water tend to have less drastic fluctuations of temperature because the water takes longer to heat up and longer to cool off than those areas without water, and that affects the air around it. Even proximity to the ocean can affect climate temperatures. Long Island, N.Y., tends to have warmer winters than areas inland at the same latitude, but spring comes later to this area because the water holds the cold temperature longer in spring.

Sun and shade are obvious environmental factors. Full sun is most often considered to be six or more hours of direct sunshine in the summer. Partial shade is about three hours of sun. Shade is less than three hours and as little as none; but there is often good light from above or reflected off a building. Many of the flowering shrubs we want to grow can take full sun. Some of these same shrubs will also bloom in partial shade. A rhododendron may have more flowers in sun, but in a shadier, protected spot, although flowers will be fewer in number, they will probably be larger, last longer, and colors will not fade. The overall effect can be greater for the landscape as a whole.

Shade limits selections. For a start, find shrubs that grow naturally in the woodland. Broadleafed evergreens generally can take shade. They have leaves all year 'round to absorb the sun's rays. The larger the leaves, the more light they absorb. Shrubs for partial shade to shade include such evergreens as camellia, mountain laurel, Oregon holly grape, Japanese andromeda, rhododendron and such deciduous shrubs as sweet pepperbush, winter sweet, winter hazel, red-twig dogwood and witch hazel.

The desiccating effects of wind must be considered, too. Most plants set in the direct path of constant winds won't be able to put up with such abuse. You will have to select ones that come from areas where wind is a problem; mountainside plants or ones with succulent leaves that can store water would be appropriate. As a rule, plants that have some water-storing capacity or wind tolerance will have either thick, leathery leaves or devices such as hairs, or coverings like wax or powder, to help keep water in the leaf tissues. These plants often appear to have gray leaves because their

pale coverings reflect light. Blue mist spirea is an example. Consider bush honeysuckle, rockrose and cinquefoil. Seaside areas present special problems, and there you'll need to collect plants that come from similar sites in similar zones from around the world for your conditions. Tamarisk, sand cherry and beach plum are some of my favorites for the seaside garden.

Newly planted shrubs may need some protection in rigorous situations. A screen can be constructed with stakes and burlap to block the wind until the shrubs become established. These screens could be left in place for the first year, longer in particularly difficult sites. You will have to know something about the moisture in the soil as well. If the site is wet for most of the year, moisture-

tolerant shrubs should be selected. Swamp azalea, Carolina sweet shrub, chokeberry, serviceberry, Virginia sweet spire and, of course, the pussy willow are good for wet soil. Dry, sandy soil is a problem, too. This condition can be altered, though, and more easily than a constantly wet area. Of course, you can irrigate constantly, but we've come to realize that water is a very precious resource, not to be wasted. Improvements should be made by adding mositure-retentive humus in the form of leaf mold, compost or peat moss to the soil. Best of all, select shrubs that can tolerate dry conditions, among them St.-John's-wort, blue mist spirea and California lilac.

The ultimate height of a shrub must be considered. Nothing is worse than having to remove a

Landscape architect Bill Wallis realizes the importance of bringing lightness to dark corners of the garden. In a border of shrubs and small trees, the variegated dogwood, Cornus sibirica 'Alba', brightens the spot. A window (right) has been treated with a reflective coating so that it acts like a mirror adding more "light" to the scene.

The tamed wild garden is the perfect spot for flowering shrubs in a mixed planting of perennials and bulbs, such as the Japanese andromeda (Pieris japonica), center right, with its drooping lily-of-the-valley-like flowers.

Flowering Shrubs for Wet and Dry Locations

Selecting the right plants for certain situations is often the key to success in the landscape. Obviously a succulent cactus, for example, would perish in the dark rain forest, and a lush-leafed jungle dweller, philodendron, would fry in the Arizona sun. These are extremes. However, around your property there are moist spaces and dry ones. Ask your nursery person, check the "Plant Portraits" chapter of this book and refer to the list below for suggestions.

FLOWERING SHRUBS FOR MOIST SOIL

Amelanchier (shadblow)
Aronia arbutifolia (red chokeberry)
Clethra alnifolia (summer sweet)
Cornus alba (Tatarian dogwood)
Kalmia angustifolia (sheep laurel)
Kalmia latifolia (mountain laurel)
Magnolia virginiana (sweet bay)
Rhododendron arborescens (sweet azalea)
Rhododendron viscosum (swamp azalea)
Rubus odoratus (flowering raspberry)

Salix discolor (pussy willow)
Virburnum alnifolium (hobblebush)
Viburnum trilobum (American highbush cranberry)

FLOWERING SHRUBS FOR DRY SOIL

Aronia species (chokeberry)
Budddleia Davidii (butterfly bush)
Caryopteris species (blue mist shrub)
Ceanothus species (California lilac)
Cistus species (rockrose)
Cotinus Coggygria (smoke bush)
Cytisus species (broom)
Hamamelis virginiana (witch hazel)
Hibiscus syriacus (rose of Sharon)
Hypericum species (St.-John's-wort)
Lonicera species (shrub honeysuckle)
Potentilla fruticosa (cinquefoil)
Prunus Besseyi (sand cherry)
Prunus maritima (beach plum)
Spiraea species (spirea)
Tamarix species (tamarisk)
Viburnum Lantana (wayfaring tree)
Vitex Agnus-castus (vitex)

shrub because it has outgrown its intended home. This happens all too often with foundation plantings that grow up to obscure views from the window. (Dwarf shrubs are particularly useful for these situations.) Another aspect to shrub selection is to find plants, especially for vital areas of the property and for small landscapes, that will have more than a few weeks of interest and, maybe, more than a single season of interest. There are many.

About the best way to learn about shrubs is to observe them, fully grown, in your area. You can discover height and circumference in books, but the best thing to do is to take a trip to a local botanical garden or arboretum to see mature shrubs in their finest condition. Or, note the shrubs in your neighborhood that look good and are doing well. If you do this frequently, you'll be able to observe flowering habits and fall color. Your local Cooperative Extension or botanical garden may publish lists of multiple-season shrubs for your particular area.

Taking Stock

Examine your property. Give yourself a guided tour of your yard. You might even consider asking a friend or family member to accompany you on your journey. When you think of adding shrubs to the landscape, your first impulse might be to go to the garden center. There you'll find many beautiful shrubs blooming their heads off. The "kid in the candy store" syndrome tends to take over, and you'll

buy some wonderful specimens only to find later that there is no place for them, or worse, you'll install them in the wrong place and have to prune them constantly, move or remove them altogether. If you just bought a house with its own landscape history, it's best to observe for at least a season. You never know what jewels lie sleeping in the landscape. Shrubs especially may look nearly worthless, until they burst into bloom. Start taking notes, and consider making maps of the property to include its assets and liabilities.

If you have a surveyor's map of your property, that will be the place to start. Make a tracing and have some copies made so that you can sketch areas that can be developed with shrub plantings. If you don't have one, borrow a 100-foot tape measure to create your own "base plan," on which you will install all your landscape dreams. Make the drawing on graph paper. Depending on the size of your property, you could make each ¼-inch square on the graph paper equal to 4 feet (10 feet for a large property).

Begin a list of what, in landscape parlance, is called the "program"—what's required from the landscape by the people who use it. If yours is a brand-new home, you'll probably be starting from scratch and need a whole range of amenities. Note utility lines, plumbing features, etc. You will want to screen some from view with shrub plants. Interview family members, too, and write down their thoughts on the landscape.

Incurable collectors (such as myself) don't always make the

best use of the shrubs. We want to possess every possible plant. But a garden of many one-of-a-kind plants rarely looks like a garden at all. It's either a hodgepodge of polka dots, or a catalog of nature's diversity. Plan before you plant: Do you need evergreens and deciduous shrubs for a foundation planting? Will you need to screen unsightly views or enhance desirable vistas? Do you want flowers for cutting and for fragrance? Is your goal season-long color? Do you want to attract birds, butterflies and other wildlife? Do you want to develop a woodland setting, hold a hillside in the sun or fill an area with low-maintenance naturalizers?

One of the things we do most with shrubs is define space. Shrubs surrounding an area of lawn define it as a place for recreation or relaxation, or just to gaze on. Shrubs can alter architecture. A tall shrub by a corner of the house can make a sharp edge seem more relaxed and graceful, subtle instead of abrupt. The look of a house can be modified or enhanced. A modern, single-level house could be smashing with low, jagged shrubs adding abstract "sculpture" to the exterior. An asymmetrical arrangement of shrubs or even a design with an Asian influence might also be perfect for the modern exterior. The shadow pattern of a shrub or group of shrubs should also be used. Imagine a long shadow cast against a wall. Silhouettes too can affect design. A Spanish-style house would look great with some pseudotropical foliage and flowers. A rose of Sharon's flowers conjure memories of warmer climates, and the crape myrtle's colors are riotously tropical. The feeling of a Tudor house might be reinforced with a staid and formal shape of a certain shrub or row of shrubs, camellias or rhododendron, perhaps.

THE BORDERLINE

A border of shrubs should have certain components that are principal to all one-sided plantings. Scale is primary: tall plants at the back, small shrubs in front. However, the depth of the planting is up to you. It really can be as deep and as long as you want, perhaps 10 feet deep and 30 feet long for a property-line planting. That's a substantial planting, and although you may employ easy-care flowering shrubs, you still should think about how much can easily be managed. Make allowances for watering, feeding, pruning and mulching. And create an access way behind the planting. You should also make a utility path, perhaps with stepping-stones, to allow you to get to each plant without compacting soil too much from foot traffic. This path will be virtually invisible when the shrubs have matured. The shrub border doesn't have to be a straight, rectangular construction. It can have an undulating front boundary. The border can pour into the landscape and ebb back toward the rear.

Draw on paper first. You can also lay a length of rope or a garden hose out on the lawn to plan the front line, or drive wooden stakes into the ground and connect them with string for a more stable line that can be observed over a longer period of time. Be sure to look at this line from all parts of the landscape, from indoors and, if you can, from a ladder and upper story windows. When you think your design is getting to look the way you want it, then draw on the lawn or ground with horticultural-grade, ground limestone—ordinarily used for raising the alkalinity of soil for lawns, and easily erased with a

---

Attracting Birds and Butterflies

Many flowering shrubs attract wildlife. Here are shrubs birds and butterflies visit for food—berries for birds, nectar for butterflies.

BIRD ATTRACTORS

Amelanchier species (serviceberry, shadblow)

Aronia species (chokeberry)

Callicarpa species (beauty-berry)

Chionanthus virginicus (fringe tree)

Cornus species (shrub dogwood)

Lonicera species (bush honeysuckle)

Mahonia species (Oregon holly grape)

Prunus species (cherry)

Ribes species (currant)

Rubus species (blackberry)

Viburnum species (viburnum)

BUTTERFLY ATTRACTORS

Buddleia species (butterfly bush)

Caryopteris species (blue mist spirea)

Ceanothus species (California lilac, New Jersey tea)

Cephalanthus occidentalis (buttonbush)

Clethra alnifolia (sweet pepperbush)

Lindera Benzoin (spicebush)

Rhododendron species (deciduous azalea)

Salix species (pussy willow)

Syringa species (lilac)

The simplest shrub borders can feature an all-of-a-kind massing of spring azaleas. Here, a clear line of demarcation is formed by the shrubs fronted by scilla bulbs.

broom or rake or washed away with the hose, if you want to alter the line. It will not hurt the garden.

When you're ready, cut the front line with a sharp spade and begin to turn over the planting bed. This is a great time to add humus to the soil in the form of compost, well-rotted manure, leaf mold or peat moss. One pound of humus, organic matter, can hold up to three pounds of water. This one ingredient is the cure-all for poor-draining clay soil and too fast-draining sandy soil. The humus improves the moisture retention of the sandy soil and opens up the clay soil so that there is adequate drainage and air (so roots don't suffocate). Make the most of your chance to improve the home where a new shrub can stretch its roots.

Planning in Three Dimensions

The "large plants to the rear, small plants to the front" concept is only the starting point. Arrange plants so the new border undulates up and down as well as along the single dimension— the line of the border's edge—or the two dimensions—the shape of the bed, its width and depth on the ground. Create a rhythm of movement that carries your eye through the planting, like waves rolling to the beach, crashing, spilling, tumbling and then gently receding, and starting all over again. The contours viewed as your eye moves along the varying heights of the shrubs will give the planting enormous impact. Color, too, will help sustain this interest. And although we are using flowering shrubs, some of the color should come from the countless shades of green-, silver- and many times, purple-leafed plants.

Consider a shrub such as the purple smoke bush. If it were planted in the center of the border, it would certainly become a focal point, but that would be at the expense of the entire planting. Try repeating the smoke bush three times through the planting. Your eye will drift from purple point of color to purple again, and be carried through the border. Never sacrifice the planting for one overwhelming point of interest, unless you are creating an enclosure for a sculpture or other ornamental feature. (In that case, you would be creating a background screen and not a running border planting at all.)

Shrubs can simply be members of a garden repertory's varied cast of foliage and flowering characters. White viburnum and azaleas star with Japanese primroses in this season's production and are secondary players in the next.

FLOWERING SHRUBS WITH FALL FOLIAGE COLOR

Amelanchier species (shadblow, serviceberry)

Chionanthus virginicus (fringe tree)

Cornus alba 'Siberica' (red-twig dogwood)

Cornus mas (Cornelian cherry)

Cotinus Coggygria purpureus (purple smoke bush)

Enkianthus species (enkianthus)

Fothergilla species (fothergilla)

Hamamelis species (witch hazel)

Hydrangea quercifolia (oak-leafed hydrangea)

Magnolia stellata (star magnolia)

Mahonia species (Oregon holly grape)

Rhododendron Schlippenbachii (royal azalea)

Rhododendron Vaseyi (pinkshell azalea)

Viburnum species (viburnum)

WINTER INTEREST FROM BARK

Amelanchier species (serviceberry, shadblow)

Cornus alba 'Siberica' (red-twig dogwood)

Corylus avellana 'Contorta' (Harry Lauder's walking stick)

Cytisus species (broom)

Hydrangea anomala petiolaris (climbing hydrangea)

Hydrangea quercifolia (oak-leafed hydrangea)

Kerria japonica (Japanese kerria)

Kolkwitzia amabilis (beautybush)

Sculptured Plantings in Three Dimensions

The transition of foliage scale can be used to great advantage. Large leaves can lead to progressively smaller leaves and then back to large again. Large ones can accentuate depth by being set in front of shrubs with small leaves. A wall of small leaves in the background would make this foil seem farther away and be a fine-textured, uninterrupted screen for foreground plantings, which would seem to come forward.

Consider perspective at this time. You may want to accentuate the length of the property when viewed from one point. Mirror-image borders that exaggerate a diminishing perspective by actually coming closer together in the distance can make the garden appear longer.

In another situation, plants can become progressively shorter.

In the first example, the planting that plays with perspective, color can be brought into play. Subtler shades of foliage and flowers, especially toward the blue end of the spectrum, seem farther away from the viewer. Bright red and white flowers are best in the foreground—they always stand out, and jump into view.

The shape of shrubs, of course, is also a major consideration when building a border. A shrub that has a tidy mounding shape, such as an evergreen azalea, might be perfect next to a fountain-shaped bridal wreath with its cascading flower-covered branches. There are many varieties of familiar shrubs called "fastigiate," or columnar. These grow straight and tall. A few tall columns of foliage could be punctuated perfectly with balls of Hidcote St.-John's-wort. This is the place to integrate needle evergreens and foliage plants not selected for flowers. Mounds of boxwoods and spires of juniper 'Skyrocket' would impose form and structure to the planting for 12 months of the year.

Forcing Branches Indoors

Branches of many flowering shrubs can be forced into bloom weeks or even months before they bloom outside. Professional growers and suppliers to the flower markets around the world use arduous tactics to trick plants into thinking that it's time to unfurl their floral bounty. Some branches are easy to force with a lot less expertise (not to mention without room-size refrigerators or hothouses that resemble the Superdome).

Keep in mind that the easiest branches to push into bloom are the early flowering ones that blossom before their leaves sprout. Forsythia and pussy willows top the list. The closer to the actual blooming time outdoors, the faster the buds will open and the simpler it will be to force them to do so. You can just cut stems two weeks before they bloom outdoors and place them in a vase indoors and mist the buds—they'll open in short order. But in order to have flowers earlier, say, January for forsythia, or to force some of the more difficult branches, follow these guidelines.

Cut long stems from late-winter to early spring flowering shrubs. Choose ones that have the most flower buds, the chubby round ones (leaf buds, on the other hand, are usually pointed). With a sharp chef's knife on a cutting board slice the bottom 3 to 4 inches of the stem lengthwise twice with perpendicular cuts— the bottom of the stem will be cut into four strips, which will expose more branch area to water. Place the branches in warm water in a tall container, so that as much as possible of the stems are submerged, in a room away from sun, radiators or hot-air registers. After 24 hours, replace the water and move the branches to a cool space, perhaps the garage or an unheated guest room—where the temperature is around 60° to 65° F. After a few days, bring them inside and cut about an inch off the bottoms and change the water. Soon the buds will begin to open.

You can speed up the process or slow it down to have flowers for a special occasion by controlling the temperature. To hasten the process, place the branches in tepid water (110°F) in a warm room, but still away from direct sunlight or heating ducts. Mist the branches at least once a day so that they are dripping wet. When the buds are completely swollen and beginning to open, place them in your arrangements. To delay opening, keep them in the cool space. Try this a few times and you'll get the hang of it.

SOME BRANCHES FOR INDOOR FORCING

Abeliophyllum distichum (white forsythia)

Chaenomeles species (flowering quince)

Cornus mas (Cornelian cherry)

Corylopsis species (winter hazel)

Forsythia species (forsythia)

Hamamelis species (witch hazel; late-winter, early spring varieties)

Lindera species (spicebush)

Magnolia species (magnolia)

Prunus species (flowering cherry, almond, etc.)

Salix (pussy willow)

A mixed planting featuring Spiraea × Bumalda *(center, right) packs mounds of interest from foliage texture and plant scale within the limited span of a garden path.*

The Fourth Dimension is Time

The balance of the planting is important, but we are creating landscape art in the fourth dimension. There is line and form on the ground, height and depth in the planting and then there is time—the fourth dimension. The planting will never be static, never stand still. The flowers will come and go, there will be new grass-green growth in spring, rich summer foliage colors and autumn color from many plants. In winter, bark texture and color and berries will punctuate the plantings and spark the always-present evergreens. In late winter, it all begins anew. With each year the shrubs will become larger, and the border will as well.

Consider bloom times of, for example, the various hydrangeas. The oak-leafed hydrangea blossoms start in early summer, Annabelle hydrangeas bloom soon after, then the mop-top and lacecap big-leafed hydrangeas and, finally, the peegee, which is almost tree size, with blossoms in white fading to pink and bronze. Planning color is one of the greatest challenges to the

FLOWERING SHRUBS WITH ORNAMENTAL FRUITS

Amelanchier species (shadblow, serviceberry)

Aronia species (chokeberry)

Callicarpa species (beauty-berry)

Chaenomeles species (flowering quince)

Chionanthus virginicus (fringe tree)

Clerodendron trichotomum (harlequin glory bower)

Cornus mas (Cornelian cherry)

Cotinus Coggygria purpureus (purple smoke bush)

Daphne species (daphne)

Kolkwitzia amabilis (beauty bush)

Lonicera species (bush honeysuckle)

Magnolia stellata (star magnolia)

Mahonia species (Oregon holly grape)

Pieris japonica (Japanese andromeda)

Prunus species (cherry, plum)

Viburnum species (viburnum)

artist who works in this living medium.

You might want an all-of-one-color scheme, one of the easiest to develop. An all-white-flower border would be spectacular, and there are many white-flowered shrubs from which to choose: fothergilla in midspring, followed by white-flowered rhododendron and azalea, then deutzia, mock orange, viburnum and lilac, glossy abelia through it all, Annabelle hydrangea, big-leafed hydrangea, butterfly bush, glory bower and the peegee hydrangea for early fall. A "hot" border would contain harmonious colors from the orange-to-deep-red spectrum. A complementary scheme includes flowers in colors from opposite sides of the color wheel, for example, violet flowers next to

yellow ones. Blue, pink and violet flowers would create a calm border planting that could be sparked by the occasional pale yellow-flowered shrub. You will have to select several different shrubs with similar colors that blossom at various times to maintain your desired scheme through the season.

The Mixed Border

Keeping the color constant by using only shrubs is hard. In an important area of the garden, you may want more color, and be willing to do some more work maintaining the planting, including pruning, planting and deadheading faded flowers. In this case you could include herbaceous perennials in the border and even annuals to fill in with

long-season blooms. This describes another use of the flowering shrubs, in a garden art form that blends the perennial border and the shrub border into what the English named the "mixed border." Here, the imagination runs free. Color can come from any plant, and forms and shapes evolve.

The shrubs for the mixed border provide a near-permanent framework for the plantings. In the background, evergreens and deciduous shrubs form a wall to contain the planting and act as a foil for the colorful goings-on inside the mixed planting. The blooms of flowering shrubs are as attention getting as the herbaceous perennials' blossoms. Massive shrubs anchor the border, define space and highlight perennials by creating a frame for the color-play between them. In autumn, the turning leaf colors of deciduous shrubs add a dimension to the mixed border when most of the flowers have long since passed. Some of these can be massed in small areas so that even when all of the herbaceous color fades, there will be plenty to look at in the occasional groupings. Shrubs such as serviceberry, heavenly bamboo, deciduous viburnum, witch hazel and smoke bush are known for their autumnal colors. (Drying ornamental grasses look fantastic with their metallic fall colors.)

When leaves drop and herbaceous foliage dissolves, berries and bark join the evergreen "bones" of the planting to sparkle with color through the winter months. Red and black chokeberries, dogwood, jetbead, viburnum, mahonia and heavenly

A range of textures produces nearly infinite variety in a mixed border that fascinates even when out of bloom with evergreen and deciduous shrub leaves contrasted by succulent herbaceous foliage.

bamboo have arresting berry effects. *Poncirus* and flowering quince have larger fruits. Besides the colorful bark of shrubs like crape myrtle and oak-leafed hydrangea, there is the effect of the varied silhouettes of deciduous shrubs seen in the winter months.

In the mixed border, bulbs and trees, vines and biennials also join the mélange. The mixed border has much more dimension than the perennial equivalent. An incredible variety of plants adds textures and foliage colors to the usual floral points of interest. Rhythm is the concept. Groundcovers, even shrubby ones, lead to higher plants; bulbs push up through the shrub cover and ivy may grow in among it as well. Colorful herbs such as sage and gold-leafed marjoram add foliage color in the foreground. Summer bulbs, such as garden lilies, push up through the arrangement to add huge colorful blossoms in their season. Mounds of shrub forms and spikes of herbaceous perennials make the planting undulate. Even dwarf trees can be included for their vertical lines.

There will be more for the gardener to do in this kind of planting than in the all-shrub border, but perhaps less than in the herbaceous perennials border. Much of the fussing is the kind of "work" gardeners love—moving perennials about, for example, or adding annuals and bulbs. And parts of this border may have to be redone from time to time as some non-woody plants outgrow their intended spaces. This can be especially true if you dare to include trees in the planting. Dividing some clumps of one kind of perennial or another will be a task during spring and fall. And there will always be the compulsion to add new and unusual finds to the collection. Interestingly enough, this homogeneous community tends to have fewer pest and disease problems than the all-perennial border. The diversity of plants means that susceptible plants are isolated and problems can't spread as easily. Be sure to read *Burpee American Gardening Series: Perennials* by Suzanne Frutig Bales.

With visions of flowers from spring to fall dancing in our heads, armed with plan on paper, we still have to acquire the living colors of the planter's palette. Then we have to learn how to "install" them. Methods for preparing the planting hole, mixing the precise medium and watering practices can be learned. So much of gardening is common sense with just a bit of scientific know-how. Learning to cope with all eventualities will come in time. I can tell you all about the mechanics of our craft, but some things can be acquired only through hands-on experience. But don't worry; if at first you don't succeed, you're bound to be a great gardener.

Flowering Shrubs with More Than One Season of Interest

It is wonderful to find an extra dimension to the shrubs that we collect for flowers. Of course, all of these shrubs have leaves through spring and summer that affect placement and design, but there may also be fall foliage color from some, ornamental fruits from others and showy winter twig and bark from others. In limited spaces, plants that can perform double or even triple duty are most welcome. The Cornelian cherry, for example, has early spring flowers, ornamental (and edible) fruits and fall foliage color. Seek out some of these versatile shrubs.

THE SHRUB PLANTING AND GROWING GUIDE

PLANTING SHRUBS

Agardener's resilience is tested with regularity by such realities as aberrant temperatures, insect invasions and too much or too little rain. But perhaps the supreme test comes in springtime, when the local garden-center yard is packed with all those plastic pots of flowering shrubs.

Unlike the experience of buying seeds, which requires imagination to visualize full-grown plants, or herbaceous perennials, most of which are mere crowns or tufts of emerging foliage in the plant-buying frenzy of earliest spring, the selection of shrubs presents a real test of will. Not only are they already of considerable size but the early bloomers will have burst into flower, and be standing there in their pots or burlapped root balls, tugging at the hearts of the shoppers with their distinctive forms, color and even the almost irresistible lure of fragrance.

No surprise, then, that so many American yards are bright with nearly identical mounds of azaleas and forsythia—big blasts of bright color bought in bloom and carried home to create an instant spring. To select only these harbingers is to miss a lot, though. The landscape will peak far too early, when in fact many of the best things are yet to come into (or in the case of the witch hazels, fothergilla and others, already past) their peak form. It is well to be prepared, then, to become an educated consumer before setting out to shop.

Foremost, there is no more important consideration than the reality of your garden. Is it sunny or shaded, and at what time of day? Is the soil mostly clay and positively soggy, or is it, thankfully, high in organic matter and therefore moisture retentive? Or perhaps it is too quick draining, sandy or otherwise dry in character? Fighting the site by bringing home the wrong kinds of plants will simply result in a waste of time and money. Plants grown against their will are fish out of water— doomed. Soil can be amended (read on in this chapter), and light patterns can be changed somewhat, too, by pruning or removal of trees, but sometimes this requires professional assistance or the use of heavy equipment that can be quite costly.

Never set out for the garden center—or even dare to pore over the stack of springtime mail-order catalogs—without making at least a tentative garden plan (see chapter 2 for help incorporating flowering shrubs into your garden design). Before shopping for shrubs, have the sites planned, maybe even the holes fully prepared or be ready to care for your nursery stock carefully until it is safely in the ground, which means daily watering and protection from extremes like direct sun and drying winds.

How Shrubs are Sold

First, it is important to know that there is more than one way to buy a shrub. As with virtually

Shrubs can be a welcome addition to the city landscape. Here a Poncirus *brightens up a city stoop.*

every aspect of horticulture, there is disagreement on which way is best.

CONTAINER STOCK, that is, plants that have been grown for most or all of their lives in some kind of pot, usually made of molded plastic, is probably the most common and easiest-to-handle form. Because container plants are grown not in garden soil but in lightweight potting mixes, the roots develop easily. Container plants can become pot-bound, a tangled, solid mass of roots in the shape of the pot. This mass will need to be scored around the circumference like pie wedges. Make vertical slices with a sharp knife about an inch deep around the entire root ball. If the roots have formed a very tight mass at the bottom of the container (and you discover this only upon getting the plant home), pull the entangled roots apart before planting, cut a disk

about ¾ inch thick off the entire base. Otherwise, the roots may not grow out into the surrounding soil and the plant will die after a year or two. In severe cases, some gardeners actually slice up through the root ball in the center and "butterfly" the root mass and spread it apart in half in the planting hole over a cone of soil.

Some of the plants sold at the local garden center in containers are not really container grown at all. Instead, they were shipped a month or two earlier in dormant, bare-root form, that is, dug up from nursery beds and cleaned of traces of earth, to save on trucking of heavy soil. The local nursery pots them up and brings them out of dormancy before putting them out for sale. This is a common practice with fruit trees, roses and some small shrubs.

Conventional wisdom once suggested tying a young shrub to a stake. The more modern approach counters this. If you prepare the soil correctly and plant the shrub in well, then it will stand up on its own. A stake will protect the shrub from wind damage, but protect it too well. Recent research shows that a plant not tied to a stake grows stronger because of having to put up with wind, and that a weak, staked shrub may actually be more vulnerable to wind damage as it grows and the stake is removed.

When to Shop, What to Look For

When possible, acquire new plants early in spring, before

the arrival of sustained bouts of heat that might threaten successful transplanting. Or, plant in late summer or early fall, when temperatures begin to decline again. Also, spring and fall are usually the most rainy seasons, something transplants appreciate in getting adjusted, and this will help minimize watering duties.

Even the best, most experienced gardeners fall prey to occasional impulse buying, such as in midsummer sales, or to buying more plants than they can set out in the garden before hot weather or winter approaches. Two techniques requiring minimal effort, called "heeling-in" and "plunging," can protect plants until their permanent home is prepared.

HEELING-IN is a way to cope with dormant, bare-root plants that are delivered too early in spring or too late in fall to plant in the garden. This technique can also be used if your plant arrives just before you're about to leave town for a week or two. Dig a narrow trench on an angle and lay the plants in it so that their roots and the lower portion of their trunks are underground. Close the trench by replacing the soil. If the plants must stay this way over winter, then mulch the whole plant after the ground freezes with up to 4 to 6 inches of a coarse mulch such as chopped fir bark and cover the rest of the plant with evergreen boughs or straw. This technique also protects the upper portions of the plants from the drying effects of wind.

Recycle Plastic Containers

Plastic containers revolutionized the growing industry, but unfortunately have left an unpleasant legacy—one that might be around nearly as long as the plants themselves. I find nothing more horrible than the sight of piles and piles of plastic gallon to five-gallon containers stacked by the garbage at the garden center. When using shrubs purchased in such containers, be sure

to recycle all empty plastic containers. Return them to the garden center for reuse, or deposit them at your local solid-waste center if your community takes this kind of plastic material. Perhaps you can suggest that your local nursery impose a deposit on these valuable containers, or better still, offer discounts to those who bring them back.

PLUNGING can save container-grown shrubs with root systems that would otherwise roast or freeze if the pots were left above ground in extremes of summer or winter. The earth acts as insulation for the roots, and the plants don't dry out as frequently below ground, either. Simply dig a hole big enough to accommodate the pot and plunge the container in the hole. Refill any crevices with soil and mulch the soil surface. Some gardeners who like to shop the late-summer sales keep an out-of-the-way area prepared for plunging and keep plants there until the next good planting time arrives.

When shopping, plan to select a diverse group of shrubs. This not only extends the season of bloom, berries and other ornamental interests in your garden but also helps avoid the kind of mass planting of a single species, called "monoculture," which invites disease and pests to settle in for a real feast.

Generally speaking, don't buy woody plants after they have reached more than half their mature size, and don't buy them too small, either. Mature specimens are hard to transplant successfully, and once out of the pot and sunk into the ground, small plants suddenly become extra small in appearance. Because shrubs form much of the backbone of the garden, buying good-size ones is worth the extra investment whenever possible.

Evaluate each potential purchase according to its structure; view it from every side and from every angle. Don't be afraid to ask a nursery employee to slide a container-grown shrub out of the pot so you can see its root system. Is it very pot-bound? Perhaps it has been in the container too long. Do balled-and-burlapped specimens have soil balls of adequate size, or were they poorly dug, having had their life-support systems hacked off? Are they wilted? Is the soil ball firm and solid? Look closely at flower buds—are they alive? Is the bark healthy, or are there cankers or fissures evident that may indicate disease? If you have any doubts as to whether a plant in the garden or at the garden center is dormant or actually alive, you can scrape a little bark with your thumbnail. Living tissue should scratch off easily and be green below the surface. A dead twig will either be brown, or too dry to scratch at all. A living twig will bend when pulled down gently, a dead one will snap (still, perhaps this isn't the best thing to do—go around snapping twigs at the garden center). Avoid overgrown shrubs whose branches are clumped closely together; they will never be graceful or well shaped. And remember, there are few real "bargains" in the garden world.

Soil Preparation

When planting shrubs, as with trees, soil preparation is especially critical. These long-lived plants are seldom moved, nor are they dug up to be divided the way herbaceous plants are every couple of years. Also, unlike the ever-improving soil of a vegetable garden or an annual flower bed, the soil of the shrub border cannot be cultivated and amended each year. Make the first preparation count.

The importance of organic matter in the soil cannot be stressed enough. Organic additives like leaf mold (partly to mostly decomposed leaves, available free from many municipal composting sites and a great all-purpose amendment), peat moss (expensive and acidic in nature, but available at every garden center and great for lightening clay soils and increasing moisture-retention in sandy ones) and compost (a blend of decomposed garden wastes like grass clippings, leaves, spent annuals, stable bedding, manure and even vegetable scraps from the kitchen) can make all the difference in soil health, tilth and drainage.

Do not skimp on the investment of labor at this stage, or on the ingredients. Too often, it is not the soil *chemistry* that is wrong for a particular plant, but the physical *condition* of the soil. Construction, for instance, or even heavy foot traffic, can badly damage soil, compacting it so much that plants' roots will suffocate from lack of oxygen. Resist the temptation to rely on chemical fertilizers to get plants up and growing, and instead create a healthy soil where roots will be able to get enough nutrients, air and water to sustain the shrub over a lifetime. Most of all, do not do *anything* to change your soil chemistry—that is, making it more acidic with something like aluminum sulfate because you plan to grow rhododendron, or adding lime to grow daphne or lilac—until you have a soil test, which can be performed by the Cooperative Extension for a small fee.

Organic Mulches for the Shrub Border

Leaves and leaf mold:
Make your own light-weight mulch by shredding raked leaves with your lawn mower or a shredder and spread them on garden beds. Oak leaves are slow to decompose and more acidic than the leaves of most other deciduous trees. Leaves gradually break down into the top layer of the soil, contributing organic material, humus —another benefit.

Straw: *Not hay but oat straw is a good all-purpose mulch, one that is widely available. It changes color from tan to gray as it ages and breaks down in several seasons. Salt marsh hay, available to gardeners on the East Coast, is an excellent mulch, and because it needs a salty environment for seeds to sprout, it does not contribute weeds to a planting. But environmentalists are concerned about the supply of this material, because it is only collected from the wild where it is a habitat for wildlife. It is best to leave this mulching material for the birds.*

Wood or bark chips:
Available bagged at garden centers or in bulk from mills (a less expensive source). The bark may be from pine or fir trees. It comes in various sizes. Large, chopped bark can be used in interiors of plantings where it will not be seen. It lasts the longest, because of its size, but it is not very natural looking. Shredded bark looks best for the front of a planting.

Cocoa or buckwheat hulls: *These are elegant, and expensive, mulching materials. Cocoa hulls are bagged in Hershey, Pennsylvania, and distributed all over the country. The shells smell great, although the fragrance fades. The only problem with this mulch is that it may mold if it is applied thickly. Adding sawdust or sand to the mulch helps. Buckwheat hulls are tiny, and a very attractive mulch, especially for small plantings. It is excellent, but it can blow away in exposed sites and become untidy or lost altogether.*

Better-quality home soil-testing kits have become increasingly available, but a professional evaluation is best for the first property analysis because it will come back to you with complete recommendations, eliminating guesswork. Then, and only then, use organic ingredients like cottonseed meal, rotted oak leaves, peat moss or pine needles (to acidify soil) or domolitic limestone or bone meal (to sweeten it). Do not expect miracles, though; even heroic measures won't allow you to grow rhododendron in the desert.

Everyone has heard the aphorism, "plant a dollar tree in a $5 hole." A similar wisdom holds true with shrubs. Dig a hole two or three times as wide as the root ball. The depth is not that important because the roots of most woody plants tend to be in the top foot or so of soil. Slightly deeper than the existing ball is sufficient. Using the soil you have excavated and 25 to 50 percent humus-rich amendments like peat moss, compost, well-rotted manure or rotted leaves (best of all, a blend of these ingredients), prepare the medium you will use to back-fill the planting hole. Spread a layer of this mixture in the bottom of the hole and tamp down.

Always lift a woody plant by the root ball, not by the stem. Cut apart and untangle the root ball (container stock) or slit open the burlap (B & B shrubs—if the ball breaks apart, that's fine, new roots will form) and position the roots so that they are reaching outward and the shrub is standing straight up. Plant a little bit high, because the shrub will sink as the newly mixed-up soil compresses. Half-fill the hole with water, and let it soak in. Then begin to back-fill with the improved medium gradually, watering in between loads of soil. Tamp down and mulch.

Don't fertilize shrubs at planting time, and use fertilizers minimally at other times, too. The U.S. National Arboretum recommends fertilizing established shrubs lightly once a year, after the first hard frost for early bloomers and in earliest spring for all others. Use a slow-release fertilizer formula that is at least 50 percent organic and whose formulation corresponds to the plant's needs. Learn to think more in terms of conserving moisture instead of watering. Realities of drought have threatened areas of the country and groundwater supplies are limited resources that must be cherished. Underground soaker hoses or drip irrigation systems get the water where it's needed with minimal loss to evaporation. Newly planted specimens may require water the first summer or two, while they get well established, but after that water only in times of infrequent rain or drought. Water deeply when watering is required. Shallow watering is not beneficial to plants, and is simply wasteful.

Organic mulches help keep the moisture in the soil, suppress weeds and also prevent soil compaction. Don't pile mulch on more than 3 inches deep, and don't place it right up against the trunk, either, or you will invite problems like rodents eating bark in winter, root suffocation or rot.

Balled and burlapped is the traditional way that woody plants are moved. When you see a shrub whose root ball is in burlap, it implies that the plant was field grown, then dug up and wrapped for transport. Large specimens are often available only in this form, acquired from sites of new development, for instance, where they were to be bulldozed, or from nurseries that specialize in mature plants. Balled-and-burlapped shrubs can be hard for the home gardener to handle; unlike small, sturdy containers of lightweight potting mix, these tend to be large bags of somewhat wobbly, very heavy garden soil.

When transplanting "B & B" stock, as it is called, be sure to remove all of the burlap that you can after the shrub is settled in its hole. Even if it is real, biodegradable burlap (much of what's used today is anything but biodegradable), any left above soil can wick water away from the roots of the plant.

Bare-root stock, the most common condition in which young woody plants are shipped through the mail, is a good, low-cost way to buy dormant fruit trees, roses and many other woody plants like forsythia and pussy willow, but it is not as successful with older specimens of flowering shrubs that have grown to less "whiplike" forms. Shipping bare root allows faraway mail-order nurseries to reach more clients, though, and if that's the only source you can find for something special, try it, because most guarantee safe arrival.

Immediately on receiving bare-root shrubs, soak them in tepid water for half a day or overnight (a five-gallon bucket is perfect for this). Bare-root shrubs take a little more patience to position in their planting holes than container-grown or B & B plants because their roots are not already spread out in a fashion that supports the branches above. Arrange the roots over a cone of amended soil in the planting hole. Water gently but very well, adding more medium as necessary so that the fibrous roots all come in contact with the soil particles.

Cut the top growth of the woody stems above the crown (where the trunk meets the roots) down by at least one-third. This may seem drastic, but you must compensate to some degree for the roots lost when the plant was dug up and cleaned of soil, when tiny roots were broken. (Fast-growing shrubs—roses, for example—are often cut down drastically.) The pruned-back top growth will produce less leaf area to dry out, so fewer roots support it. The cut back stimulates root production and gives the plants a better start as well. You will end up with a larger, stronger shrub in the long run. If the root system seemed small compared to the size of the plant, more severe pruning, up to two-thirds, might be necessary. If roots are hefty and there doesn't seem to be have been much loss, use your judgment; you might not have to remove much top growth.

When you prune at this time, follow the line of the branch down until you find an out-facing bud. That is a leaf node with a dormant bud on the outside of the plant, away from the center. The new branch will follow the lead of this bud and help to create the open form that is best for all shrubs, instead of a tangled mass of twigs. First remove any dead wood. Then remove any branches that cross or touch each other. Control the direction of the new ones with the bud choice.

Shrubs and trees can be purchased in containers, as bare-root stock, or balled and burlapped. It is a good idea to remove the fabric covering of balled and burlapped trees' and shrubs' roots.

Pruning Primer:
The Kindest Cuts of All

Flowering shrubs are an undemanding lot when it comes to pruning, because many of them have graceful, natural shapes that are best left alone. Who could improve on the weeping character of a bridal wreath spirea, which will cascade over a wall of its own accord, or the upright vase shape of a weigela?

Sometimes, shrubs will need our attention, and it is important before taking shears to shrub to keep these basic tenets in mind: To avoid losing next year's flower buds in the pruning process, prune flowering plants that bloom on the current year's growth (like peegee hydrangea, rose of Sharon and crape myrtle) before the new growth pushes out, in late winter or earliest spring. Flowering plants that bloom on last year's wood

(lilacs and forsythia, for instance) should be pruned just after the flowers fade, before any new flower buds are set.

Here are some further pruning imperatives:

◆ *When pruning to limit the size of a plant, do so in summer, after active growth has ceased for the season.*

◆ *Always remove dead wood. Leaving it on the plant is an invitation to disease.*

◆ *In general, never remove more than a third of a plant's live wood in a growing season, to avoid shocking it to death. (Exceptions to this rule may include some very old specimens, which may require more drastic measures.)*

◆ *Cut large branches back just to the collar or ring of bark tissue at*

which the branch joins the trunk. Don't cut into this collar, or below it; never cut flush with the trunk. (The old-style flush cut has been shown to allow disease to enter the wood.)

◆ *When clipping small branches and twigs, cut on a diagonal of about 45 degrees about 1/8 inch above an outward-facing leaf bud. When the new branch sprouts, it will follow the direction of the diagonal and help to hide the cut.*

◆ *Pruning cuts should not be painted or otherwise sealed with wax, tar or other material. Let the plant use its natural resources to heal.*

◆ *Avoid early fall pruning, because woody plants tend to heal most slowly at this time.*

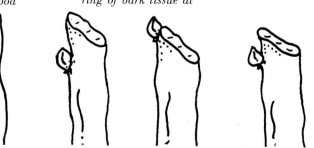

Angle the cut up and away from an outward facing bud. The example on the far left is correct. The remaining examples show cuts made at the wrong angle, one too far and one too close to the bud.

COMPOST MAKING

Making compost is simple; nature has been doing it for millions of years. The basic materials include food, somebody to chew it up and pass it through, fertilizer and air. This translates quite simply into organic material such as leaves, straw, kitchen vegetable waste (don't include meat, bones or eggs); oxygen (collect twigs to place on the bottom of the pile, to keep spaces open for air circulation); nitrogen from such sources as grass clippings (free of pesticides or herbicides), manure (my choice) or perhaps liquified seaweed and microorganisms—these animals do the work. Microorganisms live in the soil all around you. Use garden soil to inoculate the compost pile with the critters that turn your organic materials into compost.

You can make a compost pile or two in an out-of-the-way area, behind the garage, perhaps. If you make more than one pile, you'll have one "cooking" while another is available to receive more material, and perhaps, a third is ready to use. A more presentable pile can be made by using a container. A 4-foot-square box of 2 × 4 lumber with chicken wire will work. Snow fence can be made into a cylinder and placed directly on the ground, or you can buy a container designed for this purpose. Such containers are expensive, and they don't hold very much material, certainly not all the clippings and prunings from the average property, but they would be useful in small gardens, rooftops or places where the process goes on in full view. A more permanent enclosure can be built with cinder blocks forming walls on three sides with the front open for loading and unloading and turning the pile. Leave spaces in the block construction for air.

Assemble the materials before you start. For the fastest compost, shred all the organic material by running over it with a lawn mower or putting it through a chipper-shredder, which can be purchased or rented. Layer the materials in your pile or composter. Start with a loose bed of twigs, so air enters from the bottom. This should be about 3 inches high. Now begin layering: add a 3- to 6-inch layer of organic material, then spread one or two shovelsful of soil over that layer, and finally your nitrogen source. The microorganisms need nitrogen while they do the work of breaking down the material. Continue layering until the pile reaches about 4 feet in height. That seems high, but the mass will settle. The mélange must be moist but not soggy (too wet, and there are no air spaces). In periods of very wet weather, cover the pile with plastic to keep rain out (but much of the moisture in). The well-made compost heap doesn't smell or attract vermin.

The interior of the pile will heat up as the microorganisms process the contents. It can even reach 150°F. The heat will kill most weed seeds. If you have the strength and time, turn the compost regularly. This really hastens the process. Turn it over and under with a garden fork as often as twice a month. Plunge the fork deep into the pile and try to bring the bottom material to the top. The time it takes to break down the material can be as long as two years.

Don't worry if you can't use the stuff fast enough (a very unlikely occurrence). If you leave the compost too long in the bin, there is no danger that it will turn into coal, or worse, diamonds.

LEAVES, WELL ENOUGH ALONE

You probably fondly remember the smell of burning leaves every fall when you were growing up. Well, the children of today won't have such memories (but they may be able to breathe easier for it). Ever since leaf burning has been banned, municipal leaf dumps have been started all over the country. This is a great source of material for your compost pile. These places give the stuff away for free. Just think, nearly 20 percent of all garbage picked up in the United States is garden waste! Some communities have started charging landscaping companies a fee for dumping garden refuse. When ecology becomes economy, composting becomes chic.

Be sure to compost the leaves that come from the dump. There will be weed seeds in there too, so this will not be the best ready-made mulching material, unlike the leaves you rake, collect and shred yourself. The heat of the compost pile kills most pathogens and weed roots and seeds.

PLANT PORTRAITS

The flowering shrubs are among the easiest plants to grow in the garden. Unlike herbaceous perennials, there isn't a lot of coddling through the summer or fall cleanup. As long as these plants are properly selected and sited, most prefer to be just left on their own. More than 65 flowering shrubs are discussed in this chapter. They are presented with their Latin names and also cross-referenced by common name.

There is a bit of a problem when it comes to common names. They vary by region and, sometimes, one grower will adopt one name for a plant whereas another chooses a different name. But the generic, or Latin, name is the same in Pittsburgh, Shanghai, Berlin, Montreal and Mexico City. "Carolina allspice" may be the same as "sweet shrub," but a *Calycanthus* is a *Calycanthus* is a *Calycanthus*. That's the main reason for including the scientific name, but there's another. One of the best ways to improve your skill as a gardener is to treat plants as individuals. When you learn the Latin name of a flowering shrub, it no longer is just a bush. It becomes elevated to something special, something about which you are knowledgeable.

The first word of the Latin name for a plant tells you which genus it belongs to; the second identifies the species. *Syringa vulgaris*, for example, tells you that the genus is *Syringa* and the species is *vulgaris*. This plant, a lilac, is not vulgar, but it is familiar or *common*—that's what *vulgaris* means. You might be surprised to discover that you know something about these species names already. For example, *gigantes* means giant, *minimea* means small, *grandiflora* means large flowers, *multiflora* means many flowers, *purpurea* means purple, *sulphurea* means sulfur colored—a shade of yellow. There is reason, if not rhyme.

Of course, common names are useful, too. They're often very descriptive; sweet shrub tells you something, lilac tells you less. Unfortunately, hybrid names are not always as helpful. Often the cultivated varieties of plants, written as proper names in single quotes, are obscure, say, references to the discoverer's sister's husband's dog. Worse, these can be a marketing-person's idea of a sales booster. Names like 'Hot Pants' leave me cold. But whatever the name may be, having the correct name will ensure you get the plant you're after, and that you find out what you need to know from the profiles that follow. A *Rhododendron* by any other name may smell as sweet, but it might be the wrong color, or worse, not a *Rhododendron* at all.

Syringa is planted as much for its glorious scent as for its visual beauty.

PLANT PORTRAIT KEY

Here is a guide to the symbols and terms used throughout this section.

Latin name of the shrub is boldface italic.

Phonetic pronunciation of the Latin name is in parentheses.

Common name of the shrub is in boldface type.

Native American identifies those shrubs growing in North America at the time of its colonization.

Season of bloom: SP = spring, SU = summer, F = fall, W = winter; E = early, L = late, i.e., ESP = early spring

The average hours of sun needed per day is indicated by symbols. The first symbol is what the shrub prefers, but it is adaptable to all conditions listed. In general we think of light in terms of the following:
○ *Sun*—Six hours or longer of direct sunlight per day.
◑ *Part Shade*—Three to six hours of direct sunlight per day.

● *Shade*—Two hours or less of direct sunlight per day.
🐝 —Fragrant blooms or foliage.

Forceability: Cut branches that can be forced to bloom indoors, are indicated by a + for yes, and a − for no.

Zones: Check the USDA Plant Hardiness Map (pages 90–91), based on average annual temperatures for each area—or zone—of the United States to see what zone you live in. Every plant portrait lists the zones best for that shrub.

Height: Flowering shrubs come in all shapes and sizes, and we have supplied a guide to their heights so that you can judge placement of any given entry. The size stated is an approximation for the shrub after 10 years in the landscape (providing, of course, that the shrub was a fairly young specimen to begin with). For some shrubs, that is maturity. Of course, climate, moisture, exposure and other environmental factors affect size. Note, this is a general guide.

Cultural Information: All recommendations for light, hardiness, height and care are made in general terms. There is a lot of science in horticulture, but there is also a lot of art and firsthand experience. Because shrubs are living things, there aren't any precise recipes for success. We can't just recommend, "water once a week," because we don't know how large the plant in question is, where it lives, whether there has been rain this week or not, how much moisture the soil retains, the age of the plant, the season of the year and so on. Consider the cultural information your point of departure. Common sense and this book will make you a good shrub gardener.

Recommended Varieties: Whenever possible, we have highlighted certain varieties of the species listed for their wonderful form, floral color or habit of growth. We couldn't include every variety under the sun, but have noted many of the most available kinds and listed their distinctive attributes.

**Aaron's-beard St. John's-wort;
see *Hypericum***

Abelia ✕ *grandiflora*

(a-BEL-ee-a) ✕ (gran-di-FLO-ra) **glossy
abelia,** LSP, SU, EF. ○ ◐ –

Zones: 5 to 9
Height: 3 to 5 feet
Colors: White, blushed pink
Characteristics: This is a useful
shrub, all too often overlooked.
White bell-shaped flowers flare
at the ends and are suffused with
pink. Best of all, they bloom
for a very long time—most of
the summer and into fall. Very
shiny, bronze-green leaves are
semievergreen, persistent in
mild winters and southern climates. The plants are graceful,
and although rather twiggy, this
fountain-shaped habit complements the foliage and flowers.

The glossy abelia can be
pruned but it's not necessary.
These plants can be used alone
as specimen plantings, along a
low wall, or in a mixed border
with herbaceous perennials. The
delicate flowers would be welcome in a cottage-garden planting, along with summer flowers
and even herbs. Abelia could
be used for an informal hedge
in an out-of-the-way place, because of its unfussy appearance
and low maintenance requirements. The dense twigs might also
keep small animals out (or in).
Cultural Information: One of the
best traits of the glossy abelia
is its adaptability to various locations, from sun to partial
shade. It isn't fussy about soil
or moisture. Average, well-drained
soil, even somewhat on the lean
side, will suit. If any pruning
is necessary to keep the plant
in bounds or restore the shape,

Abelia ✕ grandiflora

it should be done in late winter
or early spring.

*Abeliophyllum disti-
chum* (a-bel-ee-o-FIL-lum DIS-
tik-um) **white forsythia,** LW. ○
◐ ● ✹ +

Zones: 5 to 8
Height: 3 to 5 feet
Colors: Pink to white
Characteristics: The white forsythia's common name is mis-
leading. The flowers are pinkish, especially in bud, and in
shade, where the plants do fairly
well, they stay pink. It is not
an enormously handsome foliage
shrub, and should be grown for
its flowers. Because of the flowers' early arrival in late winter
to spring, and perfume, white
forsythia might be worth growing by the edge of the path or
walk. The buds last for weeks,
swelling to become larger and
larger until the small flowers,
shaped just like those of true
forsythia, finally open. They are
borne all along the stems of last
season's wood.
Cultural Information: Average
soil suits this plant. It will need
pruning if you care about its
untidy habit. This should be
done immediately after flowering.

Abeliophyllum
distichum

Aesculus parviflora

Aesculus parviflora (ES-kew-lus par-vi-FLO-ra) **bottlebrush buckeye, buckeye,** Native American, SU. ○ ◑ ✿ –
Zones: 4 to 8
Height: 8 to 12 feet
Color: White
Characteristics: The bottlebrush buckeye is a specimen plant for a large space. A mammoth among shrubs, it often grows wider than it is tall. In summer, fuzzy cylindrical spikes grow up from the ends of the new growth. They look a lot like horse chestnut flowers, a close relative. The flowers are white with pink stamens and are fragrant. The leaves of these deciduous shrubs are also of a gargantuan scale and will have to be raked in the fall. A good way to use these plants is on their own in the middle of the lawn or to screen passing cars from view.
Cultural Information: These shrubs are not finicky as to their soil or moisture needs. They tolerate heat and some drought, and do not require pruning. Irrigation in the early days after planting is a good idea until the shrubs become established.

Amelanchier lamarckii

Amelanchier (a-me-LAN-kee-er) **shadblow, serviceberry,** Native American, ESP. ○ ◑ –
Zones: 4 to 9
Height: To 20 feet
Color: White
Characteristics: There are several Native American shadblows. This common name derives from the fact that the plants flower in early spring when the shad are running. Clouds of small white flowers bloom before the

foliage sprouts. Other ornamental qualities of these deciduous plants are red fruits in summer and brilliant fall foliage color of yellow or red. In winter the attractive stems are grayish white.

Cultural Information: These medium to large shrubs are useful in a naturalistic planting, but may not be best for general landscape use, because they are susceptible to various pests. No pruning is necessary, but shrubs can be trained into tree shapes or standards. The species *Amelanchier stolonifera*, can be easily rooted from underground stems or stolons. The fruits can be used to make jelly or pie.

Aronia (a-RŌ-nee-a) **choke berry**, Native American, SP. ◑ –
Zones: 4 to 9
Height: 4 to 8 feet by species
Color: White
Characteristics: The wild chokeberry, species and cultivars bloom in May in fuzzy dense clusters, white with contrasting black anthers. The fruits, as you might imagine, are ornamental, either red or black, by species: *Aronia arbutifolia*, red, *A. melanocarpa*, black. This is another plant for an informal shrub border or woodland edge.
Cultural Information: These deciduous shrubs are easy to grow and easy to propagate from seeds, stems or by layering. Some of the dense kinds can also be divided at ground level with a sharp spade. They are tolerant of a wide variety of soil types and have few pests.

Australian bottlebrush; see **Callistemon**

Azalea; see **Rhododendron**

Beauty-berry; see **Callicarpa**

Beautybush; see **Kolkwitzia**

Blackberry, ornamental; see **Rubus**

Blue mist spirea; see **Caryopteris**

Bottlebrush, Australian; see **Callistemon**

Bottlebrush buckeye; see **Aesculus**

Broom; see **Cytisus**

Buckeye; see **Aesculus**

Buddleia Davidii (DUD lee-a da-VID-ee-cye) **butterfly bush,** SU. ○ –
Zones: 5 to 9

Aronia arbutifolia

Height: 4 to 6 feet
Colors: White to violet-pink, lilac, lavender, orange, reddish
Characteristics: The butterfly bush, also called "summer lilac," is one of the most fragrant flowering shrubs. The aroma resembles a heliotrope's, sort of cherry

Buddleia Davidii

Callicarpa americana

Callicarpa americana

Callistemon citrinus

baby powder. The shrubs are not special in and of themselves, although gray-green leaves add interest. We grow them for the tiny flower that completely cover spikes up to 18 inches long.

In colder areas, the shrubs die back by half, and sometimes, all the way to the ground. Fortunately, the flowers are borne on the season's new growth. Because of this die back, *Buddleia* can be used like herbaceous perennials. In fact, they are great choices for the back of a sunny flower border where arching stems can bend toward the front for close inspection. As the common name implies, they are seldom seen without the accompaniment of colorful butterflies. *B. alternifolia* is a more wild looking species to look for, along with its cultivars. *Cultural Information:* In spring, cut back all the dead, dried brown stems, to green, live wood. This is one of the few instances when an additive that is higher in nitrogen, such as cow manure, could be recommended. You'll want to encourage vegetative (foliage and twig), fresh growth early in the season. Top-dress in early spring with well-rotted cow manure or use manure tea or liquid seaweed. If you fertilize later in the growing year, switch to a high-phosphorus fertilizer.

Burkwood's daphne; see *Daphne*

Butterfly bush; see *Buddleia*

Buttonbush; see *Cephalanthus*

California lilac; see *Ceanothus*

Callicarpa (KAL-li-kar-pa)
Beauty-berry, F. ○ ◑ –
Zones: 5 to 8
Height: 4 feet
Colors: White to purple berries
Characteristics: Beauty-berry is a deciduous shrub that has elliptical leaves with serrated edges and pink flowers in summer. But these are not the big attraction of these plants. It's the berries, which are so colorful that they elevate this shrub to the category of the finest flowering ornamental shrubs. In fall, purple or magenta berries line the stems. Interesting species, including *Callicarpa dichotoma, C. americana* and *C. japonica,* all have berries and there are cultivars with fruit in shades of white, blue and red. *C. japonica*

'Leucocarpa', with white fruits, is frequently found in mail-order catalogs.

Cultural Information: Not much has to be done to the beauty-berry, but it will not become a handsome specimen without some pruning to give shape. Because the fruit forms along the stems from summer flowers, it can be pruned in early spring. Some gardeners, eager to encourage as much fruit growth as possible, prune the shrub back hard, even to the ground. It *is* a good idea to at least cut back winter-killed growth each spring.

Callistemon citrinus (kal-is-TEE-mon si-TREE-nus) **Australian bottlebrush**, SP, SU, ○ –

Zones: 9 (8 with protection)
Height: 10 feet
Color: Red

Characteristics: This is one of the most familiar shrubs along the streets of California. What more could you want besides handsome, broad, spear-shaped evergreen foliage on an upright, dense shrub? Flowers? That's the beauty of the Australian bottlebrush. From late winter through summer, it produces upright, perfect flower spikes covered with stamens that make it look exactly like its namesake. Unfortunately for many of us, it is not very hardy. It is a good, large shrub for along the street in climates it accepts. It can even be grown as a tub plant for the cool greenhouse throughout the country.

Cultural Information: Callistemon is very easy to grow in nearly any soil condition as long as the earth is not overly alkaline. They are very tolerant of various moisture levels, and especially useful for their ability to withstand drought. Pruning can be done at any time, and every few years, the woody plants appreciate a thorough clipping in late winter to encourage soft new growth and ultimately more flower spikes.

Calycanthus floridus (kal-ee-KAN-thus FLO-ri-dus) **Carolina allspice, sweet shrub**, Native American, SP, SU. ◑ ○ 🦋 –

Zones: 4 to 9
Height: 5 feet
Colors: Reddish brown, chartreuse

Characteristics: Catalogs describe the fragrance of Carolina allspice flowers as strawberry-like, but I think the fragrance is actually more like the inside of an old whiskey barrel: deep, heady, not unpleasant. The deciduous leaves are quite large, about 6 inches long and somewhat puckered. The flowers are curious: small knobs with upward-facing, spiky petals start in spring and continue sporadically into summer. The color is really unusual—they are reddish brown. These odd disclaimers should not be off-putting. These are terrific plants, notably for a shaded spot. And they are a must for anyone with a naturalistic garden where they really look at home. The cultivar 'Athens', selected by Dr. Michael Dirr of the University of Georgia, has chartreuse flowers.

Cultural Information: Sweet shrub will do something in nearly any location in almost any soil, but it performs best in rich, well-drained, moist soil. Sometimes, new plants can be grown from the suckers that form around

Calycanthus floridus

the base of the plant after five years or so.

Camellia japonica (ka-MEE-lee-a ja-PON-i-ka) · **camellia**, W, LSP. ◑ –

Zones: 8 to 10
Height: 15 feet
Colors: White, pink, red

Characteristics: If the camellias were hardier, they would be even more popular shrubs than they are. Still, these broad-leafed evergreens are suited to partially shaded spots in much of the South and along the West

Camellia japonica

Camellia japonica

Camellia japonica

Camellia Sasanqua

Coast. They are, arguably, more handsome landscape plants than even the rhododendron, because of the glossy, stiff leaves that cover them from top to bottom.

Camellias are closely related to the plant whose leaves are the source of tea, but these are grown for flowers. They start to bloom in winter, some varieties as early as December (*Camellia japonica Sasanqua* blooms in fall). Flawless roselike, double blossoms unfurl from pointed buds. They can be white, pink or red and often are striped in bicolor combinations. Some varieties have semidouble flowers with two rows of petals arranged around colorful stamens. There are hundreds of hybrids available from southern and western nurseries. 'Debutante' is a pink-flowered variety with 3-inch-wide flowers. 'Herme' is a bicolor that is a bit fragrant. 'Alba Plena' is an easy-to-find white-flowered double, and 'Gloire de Nantes' is a very large (4 inches in diameter) red-flowered one. The flowers can be cut with stems; stemless, individual blooms can be floated in a bowl of water or the flowers can be made into corsages.

There are other species of camellia. The hardiest might be the fall-blooming *C. Sasanqua*. These plants have 2-inch-long leaves, as opposed to *C. japonica*'s 4-inch ones. Many varieties of this species are on the market, and hybridizers are constantly selecting more and more hardy types for introduction to northern gardens.

Cultural Information: Camellias need a situation similar to the rhododendron: partial shade and acidic, moist soil. The soil

should be covered with a coarse-textured mulch such as chopped fir bark. Fine particles in mulches such as peat moss, although acidic, may encourage roots to grow up into the material and be more exposed to cold and drought damage. Plants are usually bought container grown. Break up the root ball when planting, especially if the plant is pot-bound, as they all too often are. Some insects visit the camellias and usually group along the bark, in the case of scale, and in branch and stem crotches, as with mealy bug. Safer's Insecticidal Soap is effective with repeated applications. Blossoms are susceptible to a blight that causes edges of petals to brown, especially in wet weather. Sulfur, or another fungicide that has low toxicity, can be used, but it's better to select resistant varieties.

Carolina allspice; see *Calycanthus*

Caryopteris × clandonensis (carry-OP-ter-is) × (klandon-EN-sis) **blue mist spirea,** SU. ○ –
Zones: 5 to 8
Height: 2 feet
Color: Blue
Characteristics: These low shrubs resemble the Mediterranean "subshrubs"—herbs such as lavender—because of their bushy, twiggy habits and small, elliptical, silver leaves. In late summer the plants are covered with clear blue flowers that make it important for both color as well as season of bloom. They can be a useful plants for a spot by paved walkways and might be as successful for edging a flower border in sun and heat. The species

are not well known, but the hybrid *C. × clandonensis* has produced a few spectacular cultivars including 'Blue Mist', by far the best. The leaves and wood are aromatic when crushed.

Cultural Information: The drought tolerance of *Caryopteris* is well-known. They are happy in any soil, even nutritionally poor soil, as long as there is good drainage so the earth is never soggy. These plants can put up with a windy site, even by the seaside. Cut them back hard in early spring. They bloom on new wood and benefit from this treatment.

Ceanothus (see-a-NO-thus) **California lilac,** Native American, SP, SU by species. ○ ✿ –
Zones: 8 to 9 (except where noted)
Height: 2 to 15 feet by species
Colors: Blue, white
Characteristics: *Ceanothus* is a large group of native shrubs that includes low groundcovers, such as Carmel creeper (*Ceanothus griseus* 'Horizontalis'); such plants of middling height as the 8-inch-tall Siskiyou mat (*C. pumilus*) and giant shrubs, San Diego ceanothus (*C. cyaneus*), at 12 feet, and feltleaf ceanothus (*C. arboreus*), which tops out at 20 feet. There is an East Coast species, *C. americanus* (Zones 4 to 8), called "New Jersey tea," which is a good choice for the wild garden; its leaves were used as a tea substitute during the Revolutionary War. But most of the genus live in warm climates and are typified by the spectacular, true blue flowers in upright clusters like small, fuzzy lilacs, in spring. There are evergreen and deciduous

examples. The leaves are small, thick, often leathery, sometimes woolly with deep veins.

Cultural Information: These plants are excellent for hillsides where they will help to stabilize the earth. The plants are drought tolerant and enjoy good drainage. The West Coast kinds need sun. Many will tolerate sea spray and wind.

Cephalanthus occidentalis
(sef-a-LAN-thus ox-i-den-TAL-is) **buttonbush,** Native American, SU. ◑ −

Zones: 5 to 10
Height: 6 to 8 feet
Color: White
Characteristics: One of the most extraordinary things about this native shrub, which ranges from Nova Scotia to Mexico, is that it is not grown in more American gardens. The other unusual aspect is the floral clusters. Little tubular flowers are arranged in perfect, 1-inch balls all over the woody plant. The pompons are favorites of butterflies, too. Excluding its interesting flowers and tolerance of overly moist soil, it may not be a choice for a small yard—there are better plants for limited spaces. But in a wild, marshy garden setting, it is a must.
Cultural Information: This shrub will grow in just about any soil and will do well in wet soil. In fact, this is the perfect choice for the edge of a bog garden.

Chaenomeles japonica
(kee-NOM-e-lees ja-PON-i-ka) **Japanese flowering quince,** ESP. ○ ◑ +
Zones: 4 to 9
Height: 4 feet
Color: Red

Characteristics: These are a brilliant deciduous shrubs whose flowers appear before the foliage in early spring. The species has semidouble flowers in a deep wine color, about 1½ inches across. The foliage, green to bronze, is also attractive. Add to these features the very spiky twigs that make this plant useful as a dense security hedge, and you have an excellent landscape subject. Branches can be cut in late winter for forcing indoors, and flowers left on the plant may produce yellow, edible, applelike fruits used for making jelly. The hybrid *Chaenomeles* ✕ *superba* adds colors of white, orange and pink, by variety, to the red species.
Cultural Information: Quinces are not hard to grow. They are accepting of a wide variety of soil conditions. They can, and should, be pruned; however, they will not take to hard pruning. If you do choose to use them for hedges, be sure to leave room, because they can only be lightly sheared, and not cut back severely.

Chaste tree; see ***Vitex***

Chimonanthus praecox
(KY-mo-nan-thus prie-KOKS) **winter sweet,** W. ○ ✿ +
Zones: 6 to 9
Height: 10 feet
Color: Yellow
Characteristics: This winter-blooming shrub is grown for fragrance. Place it where you'll be sure to encounter it, perhaps by the path to the garage. The

Caryopteris ✕ clandonensis

Ceanothus thyrsiflorus

Cephalanthus occidentalis

Chaenomeles speciosa 'Toyo Nishiki'

Chaenomeles speciosa 'Simonii'

Chimonanthus praecox

flowers are borne along the stems and are little downward-facing cups, yellow with red stripes inside.

Cultural Information: Winter sweets are not fussy about soils as long as there is good drainage.

Chionanthus virginicus

(ki-o-NAN-thus vir-JIN-i-kus) **fringe tree,** Native American, SP. ○ ✿ –

Zones: 3 to 9
Height: 25 feet
Color: White
Characteristics: Fringe tree is actually a large, multibranched, deciduous shrub. Huge, foamy

Chionanthus virginicus

Chionanthus virginicus

Choisya ternata

clusters of fragrant flowers form at the ends of old wood. The individual flowers are like fringe. Sometimes extremely ornamental, egg-shaped blue fruits form but they are quickly snatched by birds. Only the female forms fruit, so you must have both sexes to get them. The flowers on the male plant are larger than the female's, however.

Cultural Information: Fringe tree is another large shrub to use as a specimen in the lawn, where it can be appreciated alone or with a twin of the opposite sex, one on either side of the main walk. Soil should be moist and slightly acidic; otherwise, cultural needs are not demanding.

Choisya ternata (SHAW-si-a ter-NAH-ta) **Mexican orange,** SP. ○ ◑ ✿ –

Zones: 8 to 10
Height: 4 to 6 feet
Color: White
Characteristics: This evergreen shrub for warm climates produces flowers that have the appearance and fragrance of orange blossoms. It's an excellent plant for the foundation, perhaps under the porch railing, where the fragrance can be appreciated.

Cultural Information: Prune this plant after flowering to produce the desired shape, form and size. Sometimes they are bothered by insects, aphids and red spiders among them.

Chokeberry; see *Aronia*

Cinquefoil; see *Potentilla*

Cistus (SIS-tus) **rockrose,** SU. ○ –

Zones: 8 to 10

Height: 2 to 4 feet by variety
Colors: White, yellow, purple, with contrasting "eye"
Characteristics: Cistus species and hybrids are plants originally from the Mediterranean regions, where they hug rocky cliff faces, so they are very tolerant of heat and dry soil and will also grow well on an embankment. The flowers are large, up to 4 inches across by variety. They do resemble single roses or giant apple blossoms. There are several pastel colors available. View varieties in bloom at local nurseries.

Cultural Information: These plants are excellent for hot climates, mostly in Zone 8 southward. The soil should have very good drainage and be alkaline. They cannot stand wet areas. They are fairly fast growing, and it is best to start with small plants. This is an excellent choice to naturalize on a slope in full sun.

Clerodendrum trichotomum (kler-o-DEN-drum tri-KO-to-mum) **harlequin glory bower,** SU. ◑ ✿ –

Zones: 6 to 8 (5 with protection)
Height: 10 feet
Color: White with pink
Characteristics: Most Clerodendrum are vines and, for the most part, tropical and subtropical. There is one that is a large shrub and quite hardy. It has dull, felted leaves that have an unpleasant odor if crushed. However, the flowers are among the most fragrant of any shrub, always covered with butterflies and other nectar-loving creatures. The white flowers have

showy pink bracts and interesting protruding stamens and pistils. After the flowers fade, very decorative fruits form that are lustrous blue encased in a rich red calyx.

Cultural Information: Give the big harlequin glory bower room to grow. It's not too particular about soils but in a moist one, it will tolerate full sun. However, it does beautifully at the edge of the woodland, on the north side of a tree, or even under a high-limbed one. This plant is very rare, but not because it is hard to grow, just because it is unknown to gardeners and seldom in commerce. Keep your eye out for it if you like to watch the winged creatures.

Clethra alnifolia (KLETH-ra al-ni-FO-lee-a) **summer sweet, sweet pepperbush,** Native American, SU. ○ ◑ 🦋 –

Zones: 3 to 9
Height: 5 to 8 feet
Colors: White to pink
Characteristics: Clethras are excellent native shrubs for a marshy area, but will grow in an average garden setting if there is enough moisture and slightly acidic soil. In summer, fragrant white spires grow from terminal buds, and in the evening, these look like 5-inch-tall candles shining in the dark. There are exquisite pink-flowered varieties that even outdo the species 'Pink Spires' and 'Rosea'. These shrubs look good just about anywhere.
Cultural Information: Summer sweet are easy to grow in moist, acidic soil. They can be pruned in very early spring to keep in bounds, but the natural shape is handsome, and no pruning

(except for removal of dead wood or faded flower spires) is necessary. However, the shrubs send up side shoots to form substantive colonies, and they can be propagated by dividing these with a sharp spade. Cut back top growth on new divisions by one-third.

Clerodendrum
trichotomum

Coralberry; see Sympho-ricarpes

Cornus alba (KOR-nus AL-ba) **Tartarian dogwood, red-twig dogwood,** Native American, SP, SU. ○ ◑ ● –

Zones: 2 to 8
Height: 4 to 6 feet
Color: White
Characteristics: The red-twig dogwoods are useful shrubs with long canes. In late spring, flat umbels (clusters) are covered with flowers, and later, blue-black berries form. However, it is the twigs, turning bright red in winter, for which these shrubs are known. There are wonderful variegated-leaf forms that can light a dark area. They are vigorous shrubs and can be cut back in late winter to produce succulent long shoots for more winter color. There are other *Cornus* shrubs for interest in

Cistus × purpureus

Clerodendrum
trichotomum

winter. Our native *C. sericea* is the yellow-twig dogwood. Native Cornelian cherry (*C. mas*), isn't known for its winter twigs, but late winter fragrant flowers, reminiscent of the witch hazels, and then edible cherrylike fruits in the fall that are as ornamental as the flowers.
Cultural Information: Any good garden soil will suit these plants, and with sufficient moisture, sun can be tolerated. They are most useful at the edge of the woodland in partial shade.

Cornus alba 'Sibirica'

Cistus × cyprius

Clerodendrum
trichotomum *(showing fruit)*

Clethra alnifolia
'Rosea'

Cornus mas

Cornus alba
'Sibirica'

Corylopsis sinensis

Corylus Avellana
'Contorta'

Corylopsis glabrescens
(kor-ril-LOP-sis gla-BRES-enz) **winter hazel**, ESP. ◐ ✿ –
Zones: 5 to 8
Height: 8 feet
Color: Yellow
Characteristics: The lovely, open, vase shape of this deciduous shrub is enough to recommend it, but the real interest occurs during the blooming period. Full, pendant clusters of pale yellow flowers form in late winter to early spring. They are fragrant. If you have space, include this Asian species. It really isn't well known or included in plantings enough, considering how special the flowers are.
Cultural Information: Sandy, well-drained soil on the acidic side is appreciated. This one is the hardiest of the genus, but still, in some winters, flower buds are killed by late frosts. Plant in front of a wall or tall evergreens so that the plants are a bit protected and so that flowers show up well.

Corylus (KOR-i-lus) **filbert**, SP. ○ ◐ –
Zones: 4 to 9
Height: 10 feet
Color: Brown
Characteristics: These are ornamental versions of the edible hazelnut. *Corylus Avellana* is a European weeping plant with oval, coarse, ribbed leaves. The twigs in winter are ornamental, especially from the cultivar 'Contorta', commonly called "Harry Lauder's walking stick," which is twisted with spiraling growth, and unparalleled among the deciduous shrubs for winter twig interest. The flowers are long, stringy clusters that hang down in spring before the leaves sprout. They resemble birch catkins—in fact, a close relative. *C. maxima*, a less hardy giant (Zones 5 to 9), comes in a wonderful variety, 'Purpurea', with dark burgundy leaves through the season. A few can be used in a mixed border, repeating their unusual color to bring a long planting together.
Cultural Information: Well-drained soil in sun or partial shade suits the filberts. They grow every which way, so pruning is necessary. You'll want to gather the dormant twigs for flower arrangements in winter, and so they can be pruned and cut for indoors at the same time.

Cotinus Coggygria (ko-TEE-nus ko-GIG-ree-a) **smoke bush**, SU. ○ –
Zones: 5 to 8 (4 with protection)
Height: 8 to 10 feet
Colors: Green, light purple
Characteristics: The original smoke bush is an old-fashioned shrub that was popular years ago and grown in many gardens. Today, the variety purple smoke bush (*C. Coggygria* 'Purpureus') is grown much more often than the species because it has the bonus of wonderful foliage color. The leaves are like coins and incredibly ornamental. The flower clusters do look like billowing smoke, and a mature specimen in bloom is a sight never forgotten. This plant is a worthwhile investment. The purple one can be grown in a mixed border or shrub planting and pruned in early spring to keep it in bounds. But if space allows, grow either one as a specimen on its own. The ultimate width will be equal to its height, about 10 feet.
Cultural Information: Ordinary soil (not too wet, not too dry, not too rich) will suit smoke bushes. Pruning is necessary for shrubs included in flower-border plantings. Although you might be inclined to try these plants in partial shade or shade, where the purple leaves would be wonderful, don't; the plants will languish. They grow so tall and

wide that it would seem to be a mistake to grow them by a walkway, but if you are a diligent pruner, they can be grown on either side of the walk and a tunnel or arch can be carved out of them as they grow up—an incredible effect.

Crape myrtle; see ***Lagerstroemia***

Currant, Indian; see ***Symphoricarpes***

Cytisus (SIGH-ti-sus) **broom,** SP. ○ –
Zones: 5 to 9
Height: up to 10 feet
Colors: Yellow, purple
Characteristics: These plants exemplify the legumes, of which the pea is the most familiar member, and the flowers of the broom are like small sweet peas. These are useful, easy-to-grow shrubs for various climates throughout America. Unfortunately, some of them have escaped into the wild, and in California, they have supplanted the wild plants completely, coming up from seeds everywhere. Although they *are* beautiful in spring when the wispy, tall shrubs are covered with yellow flowers, one escapee, called "French broom," has become one of the worst weed problems along the roadside and throughout the hillsides above San Francisco. The most familiar garden brooms are the Scotch broom (*Cytisus scoparius*), hardy to Zone 5, and Warminster broom (*C.* ×*praecox*), not quite as hardy, but a valuable landscape plant growing to 10 feet (this broom is fine for poor soil that is dry).

Cultural Information: Their success in the wild should give you a tip as to their tenacity. The plants reach mature height quickly and then tend to decline. Either keep young plants cut back or rip the old ones out and start over. The various species and varieties differ as to hardiness. Many kinds are available in flowers at garden centers and nurseries. Give them space (unless they are dwarf varieties).

Daphne* ×*Burkwoodii
(DAF-nee) × (burk-WUD-ee-eye)
Burkwood's daphne, ESP. ○ 🐾 –
Zones: 4 to 8
Height: 4 feet
Colors: White, pink
Characteristics: There are many daphnes for various garden conditions in different parts of the country, but some are difficult to grow and known well for slow growth and precise requirements. A few, such as *D.* ×*Burkwoodii*, are rather easy. *D* × *B*. 'Carol Mackie' is a popular cultivar that deserves a place in every garden. It is semievergreen and has variegated, small, elliptical leaves. In early spring, pink buds form that slowly open into tubes, then open into wide stars that are extremely fragrant. Fragrant daphne (*D. odora*) is an evergreen species with winter flowers for the West Coast and southern climates; there are also variegated cultivars.
Cultural Information: Daphnes don't need pruning. *D.* ×*Burkwoodii* forms a perfectly rounded mound. Sandy soil that is neutral to slightly alkaline suits daphne well.

Cotinus Coggygria

Cytisus × praecox

Daphne × Burkwoodii
'Carol Mackie' (right)

Deutzia gracilis

Deutzia gracilis

Enkianthus
campanulatus

Deutzia gracilis (DOOTZ-ee-a gra-SIL-lis) **slender deutzia,** SP. ◑ –
Zones: 4 to 8
Height: 4 feet
Color: White
Characteristics: What happened to the deutzias? These wonderful shrubs were popular at one time, but are rarely grown today. There doesn't seem to be any reason for this, except perhaps that the shrubs aren't interesting except when in bloom. They are excellent shrubs, however, for almost any site. They can be terrific planted with *Cornus* species, flowering dogwoods that bloom about the same time. Deutzias are related to the mock oranges. The flowers are about ½ inch long, are white with yellow centers and point to the ground. This species is especially elegant, with long arching branches that cascade like a fountain of white bloom in spring. *Deutzia scabra* 'Pride of Rochester' is a taller species with long-lasting, double, 1-inch flowers with a pink blush. Less common, it is very desirable in bloom, but because it is larger and will take up more space, it is a good choice for filling in a screen between property lines. The cultivar 'Nikko' has interesting, rich burgundy fall foliage and reaches a height of 2 feet.
Cultural Information: Grow these plants just about anywhere in ordinary soil. They can be wonderful by the street at the entrance to the driveway. In rural areas, plant them along the roadside for the enjoyment of neighbors and visitors. The plants easily root from soft wood cuttings and can even be divided. Rarely expensive, it pays to grow many.

Dogwood, red-twig; see *Cornus*

Dogwood, Tartarian; see *Cornus*

Enkianthus campanulatus (en-ki-AN-thus kam-pan-ew-LAH-tus) **redvein enkianthus,** LSP. ◑ –
Zones: 4 to 7
Height: 15 feet
Color: Cream, striped with red
Characteristics: The lovely, delicate nodding bells of enkianthus are a delight, but they must be viewed close up to be really appreciated. Because the shrub itself is rather undistinguished, this easy plant may be hard to use. It would be terrific as an understory plant along a walk through the woods. It might be useful for a border of mixed deciduous shrubs for a large property.
Cultural Information: Pruning may consist of limbing the plant up to get branches out of the way of the path, so that as the plant matures, its dangling flowers can hang over the walk and be viewed from below. They like a similar soil to the rhododendron, woodsy and acidic.

False spirea; see *Sorbaria*

Filbert; see *Corylus*

Flowering-almond; see *Prunus*

Flowering-cherry; see *Prunus*

Flowering currant; see *Ribes*

Flowering-plum; see *Prunus*

Flowering quince, Japanese; see *Chaenomeles*

Forsythia, white; see *Abeliophyllum distichum*

Forsythia ×*intermedia*

(FOR-SYTH-i-a) × (IN-TER-mee-de-a)
forsythia, LW, ESP. ○ ◑ ● +
Zones: 5 to 8
Height: 6 to 8 feet
Color: Yellow
Characteristics: These might be the best-known deciduous shrubs in the United States, and they are one of the earliest to bloom. They are overused—all too often, used poorly. Nothing looks worse than a tightly pruned bowling ball or bright yellow tombstone carved out of a shrub that naturally has a wonderful, spreading fountain shape in its unpruned form. When it must be pruned, the way to do it is to pick long stems for indoor forcing from January on. They are about the easiest shrub to bring into bloom indoors. Although many flowers will form in full sun, forsythia can be grown as a foliage plant in deep shade.

The bright yellow flowers of varieties such as 'Lynwood Gold' are a little too loud for every situation. Seek out varieties with more subtle color, if you can. 'Spring Glory' has lemon-yellow flowers on an otherwise typical *F.* ×*intermedia* shrub.
Cultural Information: Can forsythias be killed? They'll take just about any treatment, but do best in rich, well-drained soil in full sun. Prune after flowering and top-dress with well-rotted manure. Flowering is best on year-old wood, and older plants may need to be "opened up" and rejuvenated. Cut one-third of the growth back to the ground every few years, and always remove any dead wood. Sometimes forsythias are host to insects, such as aphids or spider mites, in dry locations.

Use a garden hose to spray foliage with water as a control. In severe cases, try repeated applications of Safer's Insecticidal Soap.

Fothergilla major (foth-er-GIL-la MAY-jor) **fothergilla**, Native American, SP. ○ ◑ ● –

Zones: 4 to 8
Height: 6 to 10 feet
Color: White
Characteristics: This native member of the witch hazel group has fuzzy white flowers in early spring. There are no petals, just prominent stamens. They appear before the foliage, but may persist when leaves unfurl. This deciduous shrub with round, hairy, 4-inch-long leaves is another find for an informal garden space. Autumn foliage color is presented as the sensational crescendo to the fothergillas' season. Look for the *F. gardenii* species and cultivars as well, especially *F. gardenii* 'Blue Mist', which has a blue cast to its leaves.
Cultural Information: Well-drained loam that is slightly acidic is the place for fothergillas. They are usually pest-free.

Fremontodendron californicum (free-mon-to-DEN-dron KAL-i-forn-i-KUM) **fremontodendron, leatherwood**, Native American, SP. ○ –

Zones: 8 to 9
Height: 10 to 20 feet
Color: Yellow
Characteristics: For an uncommon plant, *Fremontodendron* has a host of common names in addition to its generic name: flannel bush, leatherwood, mountain leatherwood and slippery elm. Felted green and brown leaves

Forsythia ×intermedia

Fothergilla gardenii

Fremontodendron
californicum

cover these tall evergreen shrubs. Wonderful, large, bright yellow flowers, sometimes touched with red appear through spring. It is often cited as California's native shrub (and that state is practically the only place that it is grown). However, it could be a good choice for other places that enjoy warm, dry weather. *Cultural Information:* These plants are extremely drought tolerant, and they can stand heat, too. They need very good drainage and plenty of sun.

Fringe tree; see *Chionanthus*

Glossy abelia; see *Abelia*

Hamamelis mollis

Hamamelis *'Arnold Promise'*

Hamamelis (ha-ma-MELL-is) **witch hazel**, some Native American, F, W by species. ○ ◐ +
Zones: Varies
Height: 6 to 20 feet
Colors: Yellow, red, white
Characteristics: Witch hazels comes from Asia and North America. Our native species *Hamamelis virginiana* (Zones 3 to 8) blooms in fall. The most popular Asian, *H. mollis* (Zones 5 to 8), from China, flowers by variety from mid- to late winter. Both have ribbonlike flowers that are wonderfully fragrant. The large shrubs have an open shape that is rather handsome and requires no pruning. The fragrance of these species is one of their great attractions, along with the fact that they bloom at such unusual times: in late fall, after everything else has long since passed, and in midwinter, before anything else in the garden is stirring. The winter-blooming *H. mollis* flowers last for months and brighten the otherwise bleak landscape. The leaves that follow in spring are large and coarse, but not unattractive. They have wonderful fall foliage color. A cross between *H. mollis* and *H. japonica*, *H. × intermedia*, is becoming very popular and adds many cultivars to the aforementioned species. 'Arnold Promise' is bright yellow and blooms in early spring. 'Jelena' and 'Diana' have coppery red flowers. Not as familiar is the American native *H. vernalis*, hardy to Zone 4. It is one of the first to bloom, often in January in Zone 6.

Witch hazels can be used in the landscape as specimen plants or for a background to finer-textured shrubs or perennials. They can be grown as understory plants beneath high-limbed trees.
Cultural Information: The witch hazels are all very easy to grow in any soil that is moist. Not surprisingly, woodland conditions are best—light and open, slightly acidic material high in humus content, such as leaf mold.

Hardy orange; see *Poncirus*

Harlequin glory bower; see *Clerodendrum*

Hawthorn, Indian; see *Raphiolepis*

Heavenly bamboo; see *Nandina*

Hibiscus syriacus (hy-BIS-kus see-REE-ah-KUS) **rose of Sharon**, SU, F. ○ ◐ –
Zones: 5 to 8
Height: 8 to 12 feet
Colors: White, rose, lavender-blue, pink
Characteristics: The rose of Sharons are shrubs with lovely flaring flowers typical of this enormous genus but smaller than those of the tropical *Hibiscus Rosasinensis*. They can be white, pink or lavender, often with a contrasting eye, and can be single or double. There are positive and negative things to say about these Jack-of-all-shrubs (or Jill?). On the minus side: They are not self-cleaning—they have to be dead-headed, or else flower size diminishes throughout their blooming season; the faded flowers hang on to the branches as they dry and look unsightly; the fruits are heavy and can bend branches;

they self-sow like crazy, sometimes hybridizing into interesting color combinations, other times reverting to a rather dull lavender; they leaf-out very late in spring, and you might think they had died over winter.

The good side to these plants counters every negative: They bloom late when little else is happening among the shrubs. They can be pruned hard, which not only does not damage them, but produces vigorous new growth, and the cut-back, stocky shrubs look terrific without leaves among the bulbs and other flowers that are in full bloom before the rose of Sharon sprouts leaves. The once-heavy seedpods split, dry and are ornamental through winter and for cutting for arrangements indoors. All in all, these are rather worthwhile plants for home gardens, but I think it pays to seek out some of the newer hybrids, which will add a considerable dimension to your collection. The wonderful variety 'Blue Bird' has a near-blue color that elevates it above the all-too-common kinds. The new hybrid 'Diana' is said to be self-cleaning, dropping flowers as they fade, and forming few seedpods. There are double white and pink varieties and white flowers streaked with red.

Cultural Information: Hibiscus syriacus does self-sow, but it also is very easy to grow from cuttings. This is one to plant in spring; they need time to become established and harden their woody growth to survive winters in the colder parts of their range. If you want a particular variety from a cutting of a friend's plant, mark it in late summer when it is blooming and go back to take a 6- to 10-inch cutting the following spring. They are fast growing, so starting from cuttings is realistic. A 6-inch plant will become a 5-foot-tall, well-branched shrub in about five years. You can prune them hard anytime but to avoid losing the present year's flowers, prune before June. If you dead-head them, you'll have flowers into fall. Feed with an all-purpose, organic fertilizer in spring.

Honeysuckle; see *Lonicera*

Hydrangea (hy-DRAN-jee-a)
some Native American, SU. ○ ◑ ● –

Zones: Varies
Height: 3 to 8 feet by species
Colors: White, pink, blue
Characteristics: There are hydrangeas for nearly every situation and every taste. Some are among the easiest and most reliable shrubs (and even vines). Others have several pest problems. One of the best, *Hydrangea quercifolia* (Zones 5 to 9), the American native oak-leafed hydrangea, has very few and may be one of the best all-around shrubs of all. With very large, lobed leaves, these plants will produce flowers in shade or sun, if there is enough moisture, except in the South where it must have shade. In early summer, conical flower heads form that have fertile interior buds surrounded by large, flat, sterile "bee landing pads." And this is one of the most fragrant hydrangeas. It smells of honey. The white flowers fade to pink and finally to brown and they will last well into winter. In most years, the plants' leaves,

Hibiscus syriacus
'Blue Bird'

which turn remarkable colors of burgundy and bronze, will last into winter, too, sometimes until the new leaves of spring push the old ones to the ground.

H. arborescens (Zones 3 to 9) is not very common in gardens. For some reason, these plants has been named "tree hydrangea," odd because they often behave like a herbaceous perennial. They can be cut down to the ground in early spring and they will produce tall new growth. The flower clusters are borne on new wood formed during the season. The flowers are white, ripening to green by fall. The most widely available cultivar is 'Annabelle' and gives the plant another common name, Annabelle hydrangea.

The *H. macrophylla*, called "big-leafed hydrangeas," include the large mop-top hydrangeas and the delicate lace caps. These certainly are beautiful, but they are easily damaged through the season by fluctuating weather. Buds are formed on the former year's growth—there's the rub. If there is a warming period in winter, buds

Hydrangea quercifolia

Hydrangea macrophylla

Hydrangea aborescens
'Annabelle'

Hydrangea paniculata
'Grandiflora' (peegee)

will begin to swell, and they can be damaged by a late frost. For this reason, these plants do well near bodies of water that moderate temperatures so extremes are less likely. In fact, these plants are rather tolerant of seaside locations, despite their large leaves, which you might suspect would wilt in sun (they often do) and be shredded by wind. In Zones 7 southward, they can be grown to flower reliably. Farther North, try one in

a protected spot, and see what you think.

H. paniculata and its cultivated variety 'Grandiflora' are old-fashioned shrubs familiar to everyone. These have conical buds in late summer and into fall. The white flowers turn pink on the plants and finally green and brown. They can be cut for indoors and dried, but there is a trick. Cut the stems and arrange them in a vase—without water—that's the way to preserve them. They will last for years, but their wonderful colors will be evident for only about a year. *H. paniculata* (Zones 3 to 8) is a nice plant with a blend of sterile and fertile flowers, but it has virtually disappeared from commerce in America, having been replaced by the popular cultivar nicknamed peegee hydrangea, which has a greater proportion of sterile flowers, although the heads are a bit smaller.

Cultural Information: Hydrangeas likes moist soils and acid. *H. macrophylla* will "blue-up" in acidic soil and turn pink in alkaline soil. As mentioned, the big-leafed variety's problem is bud hardiness, and unfortunately, the plants most people think of when they imagine hydrangeas are the most trouble to grow. These plants also have some pests, and that should be considered. *H. macrophylla* is completely hardy in Zone 6, but after about the fourth year in a row without blossoms, even the most patient gardener begins to think about editing the landscape. Prune out two-year-old canes after flowering, all the way down to the ground. Another reason for no flowers is

that some gardeners prune them in spring, which removes the flowering mechanism.

Hypericum (hy-PER-i-cum) St.-John's-wort, some Native American, SU, SP by species. ○ ◑

Zones: Varies
Height: 1 to 6 feet by species
Color: Yellow
Characteristics: This is a varied group of plants that includes many herbaceous perennials and shrubs. Some are low groundcovers and others are large woody specimens. All of them have yellow flowers with fuzzy stamens in the centers. For the most part, the herbaceous ones are more ornamental and have larger blossoms. The shrubs are evergreen or semievergreen. Some are subshrubs, low scruffy plants such as Aaron's-beard St.-John's-wort (*H. calycinum*, Zones 5 to 8) the best groundcover, especially for sandy soil. The flowers are up to 3 inches across. The leaves are large for the genus, too, up to 4 inches long. If the plant becomes scraggly, it can be cut back to the ground, and in severe winters it may act as if it were herbaceous. Kalm St.-John's-wort (*H. kalmianums*, Zones 4 to 8) is one of the hardiest, and taller (to 3 feet), with 2-inch flowers. *H. patulum* 'Hidcote' is a very ornamental cultivar that stays low, about 18 inches. It has smaller, 2-inch flowers that are fragrant. It is hardy only to Zone 7, and in colder areas, it is grown as an herbaceous perennial. All bloom in summer. Shrubby St.-John's-wort (*H. prolificum*, Zones 3 to 8) is a spirited native. It is not evergreen

but it has rather ornamental, shiny brown twigs in winter, with shaggy, exfoliating bark. The flowers are small, about ¾ inch, in terminal clusters. The leaves are lustrous green with glowing spots.

Cultural Information: These plants are quite vigorous, and most varieties are drought tolerant. They like fast-draining, sandy soil. Some are good choices for partial shade. As noted, rank growth can be reclaimed by sharp pruning in early summer.

Indian currant; see *Symphoricarpos*

Indian hawthorn; see *Raphiolepis*

Itea virginica (IT-ee-a vir-JIN-i-ka) **Virginia sweet spire,** Native American, SU. ○ ◑ ● ☀. –

Zones: 5 to 9
Height: 5 feet
Color: White
Characteristics: Virginia sweet spire is a shrub with a lot of interest, but it is rare in American gardens. This is unfortunate, because one of the best species, *Itea virginica*, is native to the East. In early summer, 2- to 6-inch-tall foamy candles rise above the foliage. The leaves add exquisite fall color. It is wonderful in a naturalized stand under small-leafed trees.

Cultural Information: Itea virginica grows in moist, well-drained soil. It can be grown in sun, partial shade and even shade. This is also a good plant for container gardening in Zones 6 to 9.

Japanese andromeda; see ***Pieris***

Japanese flowering quince; see ***Chaenomeles***

Japanese kerria; see ***Kerria***

Japanese pieris; see ***Pieris***

Jetbead; see ***Rhodotypos***

Kalmia latifolia (KAL-mee-a la-ti-FO-lee-a) **mountain laurel,** Native American, LSP. ○ ◑ ● –
Zones: 4 to 9
Height: 15 feet
Colors: White, pink, red
Characteristics: Mountain laurel is one of our nation's great contributions to the botanical world. These evergreens make handsome shrubs for almost any location in the landscape. If beautiful, shiny, deep green foliage were not enough, luscious flowers bloom in late spring. The clusters, or corymbs, are made up of many little cupped flowers with frilly edges, which start out as red buds and open pink or white.

There is quite a bit of hybridizing going on now, and new flower colors and plant forms are being introduced. Most of them have various shades of red flowers, such as 'Olympic Fire', and some are dwarf in stature, 'Elf', for example. Sheep laurel (*Kalmia angustifolia*) is a little-known, diminutive cousin of the mountain laurel, and it is gaining popularity as a landscape plant because it is easy to grow and very versatile. Also native, this plant has handsome rose-colored flowers in spring.

Cultural Information: They tolerate sun if there is plenty of moisture and the root area is cool, but partial shade is better, and shade will do. Being a member of the heath family, which includes rhododendron, they want an acidic soil. The addition of plenty of peat moss is suggested when planting.

Hypericum calycinum

Itea virginica

Kalmia latifolia

Kalmia latifolia

Kerria japonica
'Pleniflora'

Kolkwitzia amabalis

Lagerstroemia indica

Kerria japonica (KER-ree-a ja-PON-i-ka) **Japanese kerria**, SP. ○ ◐ ● +

Zones: 4 to 9
Height: 4 to 8 feet
Color: Yellow
Characteristics: Kerrias are terrific plants with several seasons of appeal. The species has wing-shaped, quilted leaves on weeping green stems. The stem color seems to intensify after frost and remains grass-green through the winter. The single flowers, more than 1 inch across, resemble blackberry or strawberry blossoms or single roses (the plant is related to all three), but they are butter-yellow. There are several variegated varieties. The real show stopper, however, is *Kerria japonica* 'Pleniflora'. Its egg-yolk-yellow flowers are fully double and cover the plant, even in partial shade. After their explosion of color, which comes along with the daffodils, the kerrias have sporadic blossoms through the summer. Buy this plant!
Cultural Information: Because they bloom on new and old wood, pruning pretty much puts an end to the cycle for a while, and is best after the first floral flush. The species has a flowing, spreading shape, and requires only clipping if it gets in the way, or dips to the ground, which it might do in shade. Remove dead branches from time to time. The cultivar 'Pleniflora', on the other hand, has strong, tall canes that shoot up from the ground, and pruning for it might mean division of the clump, which can be done at nearly any time of the year. Push a spade into the ground in the middle of the shrub. Lift a section for transplanting elsewhere, and cut its canes back by two-thirds. In a year or so, strong new canes will shoot up next to the replanted clump. The original clump left in the ground will regenerate at once. Little or no feeding is necessary, but high phosphorus fertilizer is appreciated.

Kolkwitzia amabilis (kolk-WIT-zee-a a-MAH-bi-lis) **beautybush**, LSP–ESU. ○ ◐ +

Zones: 4 to 8
Height: 8 to 12 feet
Color: Pink
Characteristics: Beautybush is the single species of an Asian plant that is well named. Lovely pink bells with yellow throats bloom in profusion on flat masses, 2 to 3 inches across. Later, fuzzy fruits are also ornamental. The large shrub has a vase shape without pruning. This plant is quite tolerant of heat and drought and is a good choice up against a windowless wall where reflected heat won't be a problem. A position next to a sunny wall will also allow it to grow safely in the northern parts of Zone 4.
Cultural Information: Any soil will do, even nutrition-poor soil, as long as it isn't waterlogged. Top-dress with well-rotted manure in spring. Beautybush will grow in partial shade, but flowers are best in full sun.

Lagerstroemia indica (lay-ger-STREEM-ia in-DI-ka) **crape myrtle**, SU. ○ –

Zones: 7 to 9
Height: 4 to 25 feet
Colors: Pink, red, orange
Characteristics: Crape myrtles are ubiquitous in southern

Virginia and down to northern Florida. In late summer, southern towns explode with some of the most magnificent, brightly colored, frilly flowers of any large shrub. New leaves are bronzed-red. The bark is cinnamon-colored, smooth and attractive, and the plants also have fall foliage color. If well sited, these shrubs grow into trees, up to 60 feet high. In the South, they are usually confined by pruning.

North of maritime Cape May County, New Jersey, however, it's a different story. Crape myrtles *can* be grown, but they are sometimes killed to the ground by cold weather. Still, they are root-hardy through Zone 7 and bloom on new wood as herbaceous "shrubs" that grow to 4 feet tall. New varieties are being made available that are more hardy.

Cultural Information: The crape myrtles need full sun, and in the North, in such places as Long Island, they would do well in a corner where the house meets the garage, perhaps, and with southern exposure. The soil should be acidic. No special feeding is necessary, but a yearly spring feeding is savored—a high phosphorous preparation in the South and a balanced formula with nitrogen in the North. In the South, prune in early spring to encourage new growth for flowering. Keep the shrub in bounds and create the shape and scale you want. Crape myrtles don't have many pests, although they may be visited by Japanese beetles. Powdery mildew can be a late-summer problem. Use a fungicide, such as sulfur, weekly in wet years.

Leatherleaf mahonia; see *Mahonia*

Leatherwood; see *Fremontodendron*

Lilac; see *Syringa*

Lilac, California; see *Ceanothus*

Lily-of-the-valley shrub; see *Pieris*

Lindera Benzoin (lin-DER-a BEN-zo-in) **spicebush**, Native American, ESP. ◐ ✿ +
Zones: 4 to 9
Height: 8 feet
Color: Yellow
Characteristics: Spicebushes come from North America. There are many species in the wild, but this vase-shaped one is perhaps best adapted to home gardens. The oval leaves turn yellow in the fall. In early spring, tiny, fragrant flowers cover the stems; then, bright red berries form. Although plants from the marshlands and woods, they tolerate drought.
Cultural Information: This is a plant-it-and-forget it shrub. It is happiest in partial shade in the open woodland, but will grow in a wider variety of locations. Pruning is unnecessary.

Lonicera (lon-ISS-er-ra) **honeysuckle**, W, SP by species. ○ ◐ ✿ –
Zones: Varies
Height: 5 to 10 feet
Colors: Green, white, pink, red by variety
Characteristics: When you think of honeysuckles, you think of fragrant vines that scamper across the back fence. However

Lindera Benzoin

Lonicera tatarica

there are many honeysuckle shrubs of the forest understory. Most are large, twiggy masses. They flower in spring, some are fragrant, and most have berries. Some of the species are above the norm and worthwhile for certain home gardens with room for shrubs that are a bit on the wild side.

Starting in late winter, winter honeysuckle (*Lonicera fragrantissima*, Zones 4 to 8) produces tiny greenish white flowers for months that are intensely fragrant. In milder climates, this hardy plant will be evergreen. Tatarian honeysuckle (*L. tatarica*, Zones 3 to 8) is exceptional for its neat appearance and for rapid growth that makes it useful as a quick screen or hedge. *L. tatarica* has many fragrant cultivars with various flower colors including white (*L. t.* 'Alba'), deep rose and pink (*L. t.* 'Rosea') and deep red (*L. t.* 'Arnold Red' and 'Zabelii'). Fruits are equally ornamental and colorful. *L. t.* 'Lutea' has yellow

Magnolia stellata
cultivars

Magnolia virginiana

fruits and *L. t.* 'Morden Orange' has pale pink flowers and translucent orange fruits.

Cultural Information: As long as there is fairly good drainage, the honeysuckles will stand almost any soil quality. They need no fertilizer, but do look better when given an occasional feeding. Also, pruning, although unnecessary, will improve the appearance of the shrubs. After a rainy spring, powdery mildew might show up in late summer. In years when tent caterpillars are prevalent, they may chew up a bit of the honeysuckles, but this and other pests such as aphids and leaf rollers are never fatal. Prune off damaged wood, and spray with a garden hose for light infestations of aphids.

Magnolia (mag-NO-lee-a) some Native American, ESP. ○ ◑ 🐛 +

Zones: 5 to 9
Height: 6 to 8 feet
Colors: White, pink
Characteristics: Magnolias are primarily thought of as trees, including the familiar native southern magnolia (*Magnolia grandiflora*). But many branch low and may be considered shrubs. After years, these shrubby ones can reach the size of small trees—up to 30 feet high. One native, sweetbay magnolia (*M. virginiana*, Zones 5 to 9), has waxy, light green leaves and greenish white flowers. It is unexcelled as a specimen plant when subtlety is desired. The flowers and leaves are out on the plant at the same time, and although most flowers are in spring, there can be sporadic blossoming through the summer. The star magnolia (*M. stellata*,

Zones 3 to 8) and many similar hybrids (such as *M.* ×*Loebneri* 'Merrill') are showy, early-blooming landscape specimens. They have many-rayed, strappy blossoms at daffodil time, when the familiar Asian saucer magnolias bloom. These star magnolias star in the landscape—on their own or in an all-magnolia border where similar varieties in various shades from white to dark pink can be interplanted for a stunning effect.

Cultural Information: Magnolias want a rich soil full of organic material that will hold moisture. When young, the plants should be watered, but as they become established, you'll need to irrigate only in periods of extreme drought. They are relatively free of disease and pests. Sometimes magnolia scale can show up on stems. Oil sprays when the plants are dormant are the best cure. For any fungal disease, sulfur and copper-based wettable fungicides may be used judiciously.

Mahonia (ma-HO-nee-a) **Oregon holly grape,** Native American, **leatherleaf mahonia,** ESP. ◑ ● –

Zones: Varies
Height: 2 to 12 feet by species
Color: Yellow
Characteristics: In early spring, 4- to 6-inch-tall stems covered with delicate lemon-yellow flowers sprout from the ends of the last year's growth. By season's end, blue or black fruits cover every inch of the former cluster's stalks, and these are also ornamental. But the mahonias are coarse shrubs with large leaves that resemble those of English holly, only bigger. The

flowers *are* beautiful; the bronzy green leaves may leave something to be desired. I have mixed emotions about these plants. Although they are evergreen and easy to grow, they are not the easiest plants to integrate into the landscape. It takes some special thought to find just the right place for these unique, shade-tolerant evergreens. On the floor of the woodland, the native Oregon holly grape (*Mahonia Aquifolium*, Zones 5 to 9) can be attractive. The larger Asians, such as leatherleaf mahonia (*M. Bealei*, Zones 6 to 10), can become massive screens between properties or be planted with other broad-leafed evergreens such as rhododendron.

Cultural Information: The mahonias want a woodsy soil that is organically rich and friable. They should have moisture, often present in shaded woodland. One of the problems with these plants as landscaping candidates is that they very often exhibit damage from winter burning by sun or wind. This results in unsightly brown spots that persist through the year, so consider this when locating them. The Oregon holly grapes can become leggy if they get too tall, but a simple cutting back after flowering will remedy this condition.

Mexican orange; see *Choisya*

Mock orange; see *Philadelphus*

Mountain laurel; see *Kalmia*

Nandina domestica (nan-DEE-na do-MES-ti-ka) **heavenly bamboo**, SP, F. ◐ ● –

Zones: 7 to 9 (6 with protection)
Height: 2 to 6 feet
Colors: White, pink
Characteristics: Arguably, the foliage is the greatest attraction of this shrub. It is not a bamboo, but that's what it resembles. Evergreen, palmlike fronds grow on a shapely shrub. New growth is red, as is fall color. In spring, tall flower clusters form. Buds open from deep pink to white, and it is common to have flowering throughout the summer and into fall along with the ornamental red berries that grow from it. This shrub is ideal for humid areas in warm climates, but it is worth trying it at the northern reaches of Zone 7. If it is grown between buildings or in other protected sites, it will be able to grow in Zone 6. In the North, though, it won't reach 6 feet in height; it will die back.

Cultural Information: Prune off any winter-killed growth. Soil moisture is important: Mulch to keep the moisture in the soil and also provide a coarse winter mulch in the North. If there is a severe winter, the plant may die to the ground, but roots carry over and new growth will come from below the soil if mulched.

Nerium Oleander (NEER-i-um o-lee-AN-der) **oleander**, SU. ○ 🐝 –

Zones: 8 to 10
Height: 8 to 20 feet
Colors: Pink, red, orange, cream, white, mauve
Characteristics: The oleanders are very useful shrubs for hedges

Mahonia Aquifolium

Mahonia Aquifolium

Nandina domestica

Nerium Oleander

Paeonia suffruticosa
hybrid

and screens in windy, dry or seaside situations in warm climates. In full sun, they flower their heads off. The long, lanceolate (elliptical, pointed at the ends) leaves are tough and leathery, gray-green in color. Flowers are sometimes fragrant and reminiscent of the tropical plumeria and hibiscus colors: peach, pink, red, cream and mauve.

Cultural Information: Oleanders love it hot and sunny. They are extremely drought resistant. They can be pruned at any time, but spring is best, and care should be taken with the disposal of the clippings; they should be thrown away, not burned, and never used for plant stakes. Every reference to oleanders makes mention of the fact that these plants are poisonous. It's true; they are not poisonous to the touch, but wash hands before handling food. I recently saw a television commercial for a hotel in which the doorman picks an oleander flower for an appreciative guest; she would be well advised to seek

lodging elsewhere. Many plants have various degrees of toxicity, but oleander should probably not be planted where small children play. If they already are there, instruct the children that they should look but not touch—good gardening advice in general, I think.

Oleander; see ***Nerium***

Oregon holly grape; see ***Mahonia***

Ornamental blackberry; see ***Rubus***

Paeonia suffruticosa
(PEE-o-nia suf-froo-ti-KO-sa) **tree peony,** SP. ○ ◑ –
Zones: 4 to 8
Height: 4 feet
Colors: Yellow, pink, white, orange, lavender, red
Characteristics: Tree peonies are true deciduous shrubs, varieties and hybrids of a few species of the familiar herbaceous peonies. They have woody stems that do not die to the ground in the fall. The flowers are larger and come in some unusual colors, including clear apricot, pale yellow shades and rich lavender. The floral texture is also special, somewhat like crepe paper, and the size of the flowers is astounding, up to 6 inches across. They can be single or double, and some of the frilly ones have elaborate centers with yellow anthers. Like their herbaceous cousins, these peonies will live a very long time and should be placed where they will not have to be moved—for a century or so. All the varieties

available are hybrids, most of which are grafted to *Paeonia lactiflora* root stock. The hybrids result from crosses of *P. suffruticosa* and *P. lutea*. Some of them are Japanese and others are European concoctions bred from Chinese ancestors. Among the best Japanese ones are 'Kamada-fuji', a spectacular near blue, and 'Uba–tama', an iridescent crimson. Hybrids include 'Reine Elizabeth', deep rose-pink and fully double; 'Fragrans Maxima Plena', a fragrant salmon-colored double; and 'Godaishu', pure white. Among the *P. lutea*, yellow-flowered cultivars are 'Canary', single yellow, and 'Age of Gold', a subtle golden double.
Cultural Information: Plan before you plant; these shrubs must not be disturbed. The planting hole should be prepared for the long haul. Good drainage and plenty of humus in the form of compost, well-rotted manure or peat moss should be incorporated into a hole at least 18 inches deep and about as wide. As with other peonies, planting is best in the fall, after the shrubs have lost their leaves and are dormant.

These plants can be hit by botrytis, which can result in rotting blossoms and damaged new growth and leaves. Use a fungicide such as sulfur, following package directions. These peonies like sun, but only in the early morning and late afternoon. They should be protected from noontime rays that can fade flower color and burn leaves. To avoid this, they can be placed in a bed on the north side of a tall, high-limbed tree, for example.

Peony, tree; see *Paeonia*

Philadelphus (fil-a-DEL-fus) **mock orange,** some Native American, LSP. ○ ◑ ✿ –
Zones: 4 to 8
Height: 5 to 10 feet by species or variety
Color: White
Characteristics: In a way, the mock oranges are extremely typical of the flowering shrubs. They are a woody deciduous plants that usually grow to about 10 feet (although there are smaller cultivated varieties available). Single or double flowers form along with the roses in late spring to early summer. They are white, with nectar-filled centers, and yellow anthers showing on the singles, obscured by frilly petals on the doubles. They last a short time, only about two weeks. For the rest of the season, fresh green leaves cover the large shrubs. They are invaluable for creating property screens where they do not require pruning, except for the removal of dead wood, if you get around to it. They would be good along the driveway if it is against the property line, as so many driveways are. There are about 50 available varieties from which to choose at nurseries and through mail-order sources. *Philadelphus coronarius*, the common mock orange, a familiar species, is still available. Seek out new varieties of single or doubles, as they are often superior to older hybrids. Try the double *P. ×virginalis*, for example, which itself comes in varieties such as 'Albâtre' and 'Argentine'. The double-flowered kinds hold their petals longer than the singles. Some of the

Philadelphus
coronarius

best cultivars include *P. ×lemoinei* 'Boule d'Argent', large double flowers and somewhat fragrant; *P. ×cymosus* 'Conquête', one of the most fragrant of the singles; *P. ×lemoinei* 'Innocence', with slightly smaller flowers but in ample clusters is also intensely fragrant; 'Frosty Morn', perhaps the most hardy and *P. coronarius* 'Aureus', a cultivar whose new foliage is bright golden green.
Cultural Information: These shrubs are easy to grow. They are not particular as to soil. Because they bloom on new wood, they could be sheared just after flowering. Some of the varieties are arching, almost fountain shaped. These will need pruning to keep them in shape.

Pieris japonica (PY-eer-is ja-PON-i-ka) **Japanese andromeda,**

Japanese pieris, lily-of-the-valley shrub, ESP. ◑ –
Zones: 5 to 8 (4 with protection)
Height: 4 to 8 feet
Colors: White, pink
Characteristics: Japanese pieris would be known as an ornamental evergreen for hedges and

Pieris japonica *'Valley Rose'*

Pittosporum Tobira *'Variegata'*

Pittosporum Tobira (pit-TOSS-por-um to-Bl-ra) **pittosporum,** SP. ○ ◑ 🐞 –
Zones: 8 to 10
Height: 6 feet
Color: White
Characteristics: Pittosporums are evergreen woody shrubs with 2- to 3-inch-long elliptical leaves with a distinct midrib. They have a wonderful, mounding shape with little or no pruning, and there is a variegated variety, *Pittosporum Tobira* 'Variegata', with gray-green leaves marked with white. They would be noted only as evergreens except for the flowers. Substantial clusters of white stars that fade to gold cover all the tips of last season's growth. They are intensely fragrant. This plant is not very hardy, but in areas where it can be grown, it should be.
Cultural Information: This imported shrub from Japan is easy to grow. Hot, sandy sites are fine, even when soil conditions are dry. It can be grown by the seaside in Bermuda, but is equally at home in a protected spot, away from sun, in Seattle. It also makes an excellent tub plant for a cool room or greenhouse, in which case, it would love to spend the summer in its pot in a sheltered spot outdoors.

Poncirus trifoliata (pon-SEER-us try-fo-lee-AH-ta) **trifoliate orange, hardy orange,** SP. ○ ◑ 🐞 –
Zones: 6 to 9
Height: 10 feet
Color: White
Characteristics: The hardy trifoliate orange is actually a citrus

screens only, if but for the beautiful flowers. In early spring, long drooping clusters of bell-like flowers cover this plant. The flowers are usually white with golden bracts, but there are cultivars, such as 'Valley Rose', 'Flamingo' and 'Wada', with pink flowers. These plants are hardy, but a protected spot might be advisable in northern climates, because the flower buds can be damaged by a surprise late frost. The new growth on some cultivars is vivid red, 'Forest Flame' and 'Mountain Fire', for example. This effect is interesting, but not too subtle, and the fact that these varieties will stand out from the crowd should be noted. Dwarf varieties can be used in a rock garden. All are slow growing and would be suitable for an entry planting. There are other species, including a native, mountain pieris, or mountain andromeda (*P. floribunda*).
Cultural Information: Heath plants, *Pieris* species want acidic soil that is moist with lots of organic material. The shrub will stand sun, but if the atmosphere and soil are dry, red spider mites may visit. They can be controlled with Safer's Insecticidal Soap in repeated applications, but it is far better to provide an environment that is more favorable to the shrubs and less to the liking of the mites.

that produces real fruits in cold climates. Rich, dark green, three-part leaves grow all over these deciduous shrubs. They have 1-inch single flowers in spring that are fragrant but don't challenge subtropical varieties. The fruits are wonderfully ornamental in fall, fuzzy, like peaches, and about 1½ inches in diameter. They can be used for marmalade or as a garnish for drinks but are too sour to eat fresh off the shrub.

This may be one of the best plants to use as a security hedge— it has 1-inch-long thorns. The spear-covered branches will go all the way to the ground if unpruned, or on sheared specimens, but *Poncirus* can also be limbed up as it grows to make a magnificent "standard," a lollipop- or tree-shaped topiary. It has lovely striped bark.
Cultural Information: Well-drained, acidic soil is all that is needed for these shrubs that can, but infrequently do, reach 20 feet in height. These plants are rarely offered in nurseries. Some mail-order companies offer small plants. But if you know where one grows, you can collect fruits, because it is simple to grow these shrubs from seeds. Store fruits in the refrigerator for a few months and then cut open to remove seeds, which can be sown in any houseplant medium in a sunny window. Fruits that drop and remain on the ground through the winter may also be a source for "stratified" seeds—those exposed to chilling and warming. (In order to germinate, some seeds of hardy plants need a period of chilling to break the seeds' dormancy.)

Poncirus trifoliata

Potentilla fruticosa (po-ten-TILL-a froo-ti-KO-sa) **cinque-foil**, some Native American, SU. ○ –
Zones: 2 to 7
Height: 1 to 5 feet
Color: Yellow
Characteristics: This is a large group of shrubby plants. Some run along the ground, others are herbaceous. The ones that we want to learn about are, of course, medium-size woody shrubs. *Potentilla fruticosa* is one of the few species found all over the northern hemisphere. They are small, 1 to 5 feet high, and twiggy with small leaves and numerous yellow, single-roselike flowers in clusters. There are about 40 varieties with varying pale colors. They are principally used for low hedges

Potentilla *'Gold Drop'*

or as groundcovers and look well along a low wall or as a curbside planting.

Cultural Information: Cinquefoils would be good next to the lawn, because they need similar conditions: full sun, clayey but well-drained soil, and alkalinity. Sometimes older shrubs tend to flop open, leaving a dead area in the center. Severe pruning, back by one-third, will rejuvenate older plants.

Prunus glandulosa

Prunus (PROO-nus) **flowering-cherry, -almond, -plum,** SP. ○ ◐ ❋ +

Zones: Varies

Height: Varies

Colors: Pink, white

Characteristics: Cherries, peaches, almonds, plums, all are members of the *Prunus* genus. Some are ornamental shrubs, such as the dwarf flowering almond, *P. glandulosa,* hardy in Zones 4 to 8. Numerous pink or white flowers cover the stems before the foliage sprouts. The sand cherry (*P. Besseyi*) is a medium-size shrub up to 6 feet that is hardy to Zone 4. Small flowers bloom in clusters in spring, and it produces small black, edible, sweet fruits that are often used for jelly. *P.* × *cistena* is the purple-leaf sand cherry. It adds colorful foliage to the same qualities as the preceding ornamental, and it is hardy in Zones 2 to 8. The cherry laurel, *P. Laurocerasus,* isn't as hardy (Zone 7; 6 with protection), but it is evergreen. It is extremely ornamental and there are several cultivars. This plant tolerates partial shade, and some of the varieties, 'Otto Luyken', for example, can grow in shade.

Cultural Information: Except where noted, these flowering plants are deciduous and need full sun. They all like very well drained soil. Some insect infestations may occur. Prune out and destroy damaged wood. Try Safer's Insecticidal Soap.

Pussy willow; see *Salix*

Quince, Japanese flowering; see *Chaenomeles*

Raphiolepis indica (ra-fi-OL-ep-is IN-di-ka) **Indian hawthorn,** SP. ○ ◐ –

Zones: 8 to 10

Height: 4 feet

Color: Pink

Characteristics: Indian hawthorn is not the hardiest plant, but it is rather forgiving in the zones that it likes. It makes an excellent city shrub, even along a busy street or highway. It won't need watering there, either. It is evergreen, with interesting small leaves, but the flowers are the best part. Full clusters of rich pink flowers cover the shrubs through most of spring.

Cultural Information: Easily grown in most soils. Best flowering occurs in sun, but it will do quite well in partial shade.

Red-twig dogwood; see *Cornus*

Redvein enkianthus; see *Enkianthus*

Rhododendron (ro-do-DEN-dron) **rhododendron, azalea, rose bay,** ESP, SP, SU by species. ○ ◐ ● ❋ –

Zones: Varies

Height: 1 to 20 feet by species

Colors: All except true blue

Characteristics: One could easily write a book on *Rhododendron* alone, and many authors have. Included in this group are large, tropical evergreens with enormous leaves, the familiar large evergreens, deciduous woody specimens often called azaleas, and tiny-leafed evergreen azaleas that grow in nearly every suburban landscape in the United States. Most of the ones known best as rhododendron have large, flat, bell-shaped flowers. The azaleas have flowers that are more funnel or trumpet shaped. Some individuals in each of these groups are fragrant, a few are not. Some bloom in late winter to early spring, and one Native American, *Rhododendron prunifolium*, blooms mid- to late summer. It would be impossible to name all of the hundreds of species and varieties here, but some of the best are worth noting individually.

Of the large-leafed evergreens, *R. catawbiense* (Zones 4 to 8) and its hybrids are about the most reliable. They are very hardy and even somewhat drought tolerant—unusual for these moisture lovers. This late–spring-blooming plant is also native. The species has unpretentious, dull lilac flowers, but lots of them. They should be deadheaded for the most bloom the following year. This native is from the American southeast. Rose bay rhododendron (*R. maximum*, Zones 4 to 8) is another southeastern American native. It flowers from late spring to early summer. In cultivation since 1736, it is popular because it adapts better to deeper shade than most.

To keep in moisture, the leaves have an unusual self-preservation device. When the temperature drops below freezing, the leaves curl. You can almost tell the temperature by looking out your window at the "rhodies." When it's really cold, the shrubs look as if they're covered with cigars.

One of the earliest spring bloomers is the P.J.M. hybrid, an evergreen variety that is a rich purple, named for the developer, Peter John Mezitt of Weston Nurseries in Hopkinton, Massachusetts. P.J.M. doesn't set seed often, so it directs its energy toward flower bud production and is a profuse bloomer. There is also a white one due on the market soon. These were developed from the native Carolina rhododendron (*R. carolinianum*, crossed with *R. dauricum sempervirens*), which comes from the Blue Ridge Mountains. It is very compact and floriferous. At maturity it forms a perfect mound 6 feet high and 7 feet wide in Zones 4 to 8.

Among the best of the Asian members of the genus is *R. Fortunei*. Its hybrids are magnificent for flower lovers. The individual flowers can be up to 3½ inches wide in trusses (compact flower clusters) of up to 12. The flowers are usually pink to lilac, sometimes with streaks of white or yellow. The species likes warmth. Floridian gardeners take heart, this is one of the best for Zones 8 and 9. Nevertheless, it does just fine north to Zone 6, and the hybrids are often hardier. Perhaps the most wonderful is 'Scintillation', which has a veritable sunset of colors in its flowers. It is a dependable and hardy subject, available each spring at nearly every garden center and nursery.

A somewhat recently introduced Asian species, *R. yakusimanum* (Zone 5), is being used to develop hybrids that will be introduced over the next few decades. This is always one of the stars of the collector's garden. Very shiny green leaves are covered on the undersides

Raphiolepis indica

Rhododendron *hybrids*

Rhododendron *Kurume hybrids*

Rhododendron

R. arborescens is called sweet azalea (Zones 4 to 8) and is native to moist areas from Pennsylvania south to Georgia. Another common name for this plant is tree azalea, which should tell you to give this plant ample room to grow. From Kentucky southeast to Georgia comes *R. Bakeri* (Zones 5 to 7). It and its hybrids are particularly good in shade. After the plants have leafed-out, red, orange or yellow flowers with a yellow-orange blotch appear. Flame azalea (*R. calendulaceum*, Zones 5 to 8) blooms late, and it was one of the plants for the Ghent and Exbury hybrids.

R. periclymenoides, called pinxterbloom or wild honeysuckle (Zones 3 to 8), can tolerate dry locations with sandy soil. The flowers are purple to pale pink and have very long stamens. It grows from the coast of Maine down to South Carolina and Tennessee. It also parented some of the Ghent hybrids, and the common name comes from what the Dutch call *Pingsterbloem*. *R. prinophyllum* (Zones 3 to 8) resembles the former, but the undersides of the leaves are hairy and the flowers lily- and spice-scented. It leafs-out and blooms early for azaleas; in fall, their foliage turns scarlet. The flowers bloom in a full range of pink shades. This plant is indigenous from Quebec to Oklahoma.

R. Vaseyi is the pinkshell azalea (Zones 4 to 8) from North Carolina swamps; it is remarkably adaptable, even to a dry location. Deep green, 5-inch-long leaves turn crimson in fall. In midspring, before the

with thick brown or white hairs that feel like felt. Large bunches of bell-shaped pink or white flowers bloom in spring. The small, mounded shrubs grow only to about 3 feet by 3 feet after 10 years.

Many of the deciduous rhododendron, usually called azaleas, come from North America. Yellow shades and tints are not uncommon in these plants—from flame orange to chrome yellow to pale primrose. Consider these species and look for some of the hundreds of hybrids with incredible floral colors. Many have fall foliage color as well.

foliage appears, unscented gossamer blossoms of pale pink to rose with sienna speckles bloom.

The spicy fragrance of the swamp azalea (*R. viscosum*, Zones 3 to 9) is wonderful. Trumpet flowers in the palest pink to white come in early summer—July in Zone 6, the middle of its Zone 3 to 9 range. This native shrub has a very fragile, lacy pattern of growth that complements its pale flower clusters.

The royal azalea (*R. Schlippenbachii*), a native of Manchuria, Korea and Japan, looks at home everywhere (Zones 4 to 7). This is one of the most popular deciduous azaleas and should top the list of those new to these plants.

When you go to the garden center in spring, don't snatch up the first tiny-leaf evergreen azaleas in bright orange and magenta. These are easy to grow and dependable, but you'll just end up with a mirror-image landscape that is no different from your neighbors' to the left or right. Seek out instead some of these incredibly varied and spectacular species and hybrids, and many more that cannot be covered in any space limited to under 2,000 pages. Look also to the color catalogs for pictures of plants such as: *R. × gandavense*, Knap Hill and Exbury hybrids and *R. × Kosteranum* (Zones 5 to 7).

Cultural Information: The evergreen rhododendron make good shrub choices for city gardens. Their shiny leaves wash clean in rain storms, and they are tolerant of air pollution. Because of their shallow roots, they transplant well. They benefit from being placed among other plants, as long as there is little root competition. Mulch is a must, however, and it should be a coarse-textured one, such as shredded pine bark.

Most available rhododendron are field grown, that is, they are planted and grown in the open sun and heavily irrigated. This is unfortunate, for you will buy a very compact, densely branched specimen that will not end up looking like that in the shaded garden. Also, it tends to be a shock to the young plants when you set them into the garden. And they will take some time to come back—sometimes years before they go back into the flowering mode. Have patience and you will be rewarded.

When planting the "rhodie," be sure to incorporate a good deal of organic matter, especially into the top foot of soil, because that is where much of the root system will live. Dig a hole about twice as deep and twice as wide as the container or burlap-covered root ball. Enrich the excavated soil with compost, well-rotted cow manure, leaf mold or the ever-available peat moss.

Rhodotypos scandens

(ro-do-TY-pus skan-DENZ) **jetbead**, SP. ○ ◑ ● –
Zones: 4 to 8
Height: 4 to 6 feet
Color: White
Characteristics: Jetbead is a little-known plant that should be grown more often. It has 2-inch, single white flowers similar to those of a rose. The white flowers and general habit also resemble kerria. Later, black, cherrylike fruits hang from the stems.

Cultural Information: Jetbead is a very natural-looking plant and would be nice for a wild garden. It is, nevertheless, very tolerant of pollution and harsh city conditions and is just as at home in the concrete jungle as in the wild country. Sun and dense shade are both acceptable.

Rhododendron prunifolium

Rhododendron maximum

Rhodotypos scandens

Ribes sanguineum (Ribes *calyx after petal drop*)

Ribes sanguineum *'China Rose'*

does produce ornamental fruit in late summer that is blue-black and glaucus—covered with a powdery bloom like an Italian plum.

Cultural Information: Ribes is easy to grow and usually presents few problems. It can be attacked by aphids and Japanese beetles, and some of the other predators that go after fruiting crops. But it will grow in sun or shade, and is worth trying when you find it at the nursery or in mail-order catalogs.

Rockrose; see *Cistus*

Rose bay; see *Rhododendron*

Rose of Sharon; see *Hibiscus*

Ribes sanguineum (REE-beez sang-GWIN-ee-um) **flowering currant**, Native American, SP. ○ ◑ ●
Zones: 6 to 8
Height: 5 to 10 feet
Color: Red
Characteristics: The flowering currant is related to the gooseberry and edible red and black currants. They have beautiful hanging flowers in early spring and lovely green ribbed, felted leaves. Although this was at one time a very popular landscape plant, you don't see it very often today. The only possible reason is that currants in general have been banished because some of them are the alternate host of white pine disease. This is not the case with this ornamental. In Europe, you'll find this plant and various cultivars widely grown, and there it is an import from the West Coast. It

Rubus (ROO-bus) **ornamental blackberry**, some Native American, LSP. ○ ◑ –
Zones: Varies
Height: 5 feet
Colors: White, pink
Characteristics: These are ornamental relatives of the raspberries and blackberries, and although they are common in European gardens, they are not often grown in America. However, being also related to roses, they have lovely flowers. *Rubus odoratus* is a North American native, hardy to Zone 3. This one is an upright shrub with raspberry red to purple flowers from late spring to summer. It has practically no thorns, but does have fruits, although they are inedible. *R. × tridel* 'Benenden', hardy to Zone 6, is the one that is most popular in Europe. It is often grown in an

all-white-flowered border among roses, lilacs and iris.

Cultural Information: These plants are easy to grow; just cut out dead wood. *R. × tridel* 'Benenden' seems to grow in a similar way to the canning fruits to which it is related, that is, the 2-year-old wood blooms and then dies, and these canes should be removed in the spring once you can determine that they have died and dried, turning brown. It is quite easy to tell the faded wood from new and second-year growth.

St.-John's-wort; see *Hypericum*

Salix (SAY-licks) **pussy willow**, LW. ◑ –
Zones: Varies
Height: 10 feet
Color: Gray
Characteristics: There are willows from all over the world. More than 300 species are known. There are tiny shrubs that hug rocky cliff faces in the wild and many more from marshlands in the cooler parts of the temperate world. We grow the ones that produce ornamental catkins, the pussies. The most familiar is the common pussy willow (*Salix discolor*). It has long canes that are wonderful to cut and bring indoors in midwinter to force into bloom. The more you cut it, the nicer the canes will be; in fact, cut it down near the ground every so often. One of the most hardy, it grows to Zone 3. *S. discolor* 'Melanostchys' is the black pussy willow, hardy to Zone 5. Its catkins are truly black. Rosegold pussy willow

Rubus odoratus

Salix gracilistyla

Salix gracilistyla

(*S. gracilistyla*) has the most elegant catkins in a wonderful feline gray color. The male catkins of this shrub, which can grow to Zone 6, show pink to rose as they grow. Many are produced and they are large. *S. sachalinensis* 'Sekka' from Japan has twisted, flat branches as it matures. The branches are fantastic cut for indoors. Its contorted twigs form on a plant that has a rather nice vase shape. It is hardy to Zone 5.

Cultural Information: Pussy willows like a very moist location, but will thrive anywhere within their zone, and they are among the easiest shrubs to grow. They are very rewarding plants for beginners, although they can grow out of bounds in the landscape. Cut stems will root readily in water, and in fact, the willow water possesses properties that induce rooting in other plants. Place cuttings of ivy or other water-rooting plantings in willow water, and they will sprout roots faster.

Serviceberry; see ***Amelanchier***

Shadblow; see ***Amelanchier***

Slender deutzia; see ***Deutzia***

Smoke bush; see ***Cotinus***

Snowberry; see ***Symphoricarpos***

Sorbaria sorbifolia (sorBAIR-ee-a sor-bi-FO-lee-a) **false spirea,** SU. ◑ –
Zones: 2 to 7
Height: 6 feet
Color: White
Characteristics: False spirea is a plant for the waste places, and in fact, can often be seen naturalizing along the highways and roadsides. Still and all, this might be a good choice for summer bloom in just such situations, perhaps for the unpaved road to a second home in a rural setting. In a wild garden, it does have a place.
Cultural Information: These plants need space, and they do spread. They like rich, moist soil, but as you might imagine, will put up with just about anything.

Spicebush; see ***Lindera***

Spirea, false; see ***Sorbaria***

Sorbaria sorbifolia

Spiraea (spy-REE-a) **spirea,**
SP, SU. ○ ◑ ● –
Zones: 3 to 8
Height: 3 to 5 feet
Colors: White, pink, red
Characteristics: This is an enormously useful group of deciduous ornamental, flowering shrubs, from spring's bridal wreath with its arching stems covered with white flower tufts (*Spiraea × Vanhouttei*), to summer's *S. × Bumalda* with flat clusters of rose-pink flowers. And there are dwarf species as well. *S. albiflora* (Zones 4 to 8) is the Japanese white spirea—only 18 inches tall. Look for the chartreuse-colored leaves of *S. × Bulmalda*, 'Gold Flame'; *S. × Bulmalda* 'Shibori', has white and rose-pink flowers on the same plant. The most common variety is *S. × Bulmalda* 'Anthony Waterer'. Most of the other spireas have white flowers in a usual button form. There is a dwarf bridal wreath, 'Swan Lake', for example.

Cultural Information: Ordinary garden soil suits. Nearly all of these plants can be pruned. The arching stems of the spring-blooming whites should be pruned just after flowering. Some of the summer-blooming, rose-red kinds and ones with interesting foliage benefit from being almost sheared in late winter. New growth will be vigorous and leaves, lush. Cut them back to about 10 inches from the ground.

Spirea; see ***Spiraea***

Summer sweet; see ***Clethra***

Sweet pepperbush; see ***Clethra***

Sweet shrub; see ***Calycanthus***

Spiraea prunifolia

Spiraea × Bumalda *'Gold Flame'*

Spiraea × Bumalda

Symphoricarpos albus

Syringa vulgaris
Hybrid

Syringa vulgaris Hybrid

Sweet spire, Virginia; see
Itea

Symphoricarpos (sim-for-i-
KAR-pos) **snowberry, Indian
currant, coralberry**, SP, SU.
◑ –

Zones: 3 to 7
Height: 4 feet
Colors: White, pink
Characteristics: Symphoricarpos
shrubs are not grown for their
flowers at all, although they are
related to the honeysuckles.
They have incredibly ornamental fruits. These oddities are
wonderful for wild gardens, but
be sure to place the arching
stems where the fruit, which is
usually carried on the ends of
the branches, can be viewed
up close and touched. Snowberry (*S. albus*) have fruits that
are about the size of marbles
and pure white. They are squishy
and unfortunately don't dry, but
are good cut for fresh arrangements. The gray leaves are mod-
erately attractive, but the plant's
habit is not special. Indian currant or coralberry (*S. orbiculatus*)
has long-lasting red fruits and
fall foliage interest as well. The
cultivar 'Leucocarpus' has yellow flowers and white fruits.
This is also a plant for the wild
garden.
Cultural Information: Poor soil
and partial shade are fine for
snowberry. Very hardy (to Zone
3), these are good plants for the
Midwest and will even stand
Chicago winters and summers
easily.

Syringa (sir-RING-a) **lilac**, SP.
○ ✿ –
Zones: Varies
Height: 5 to 20 feet by species
Colors: White, pink, lavender,
red, blue

Characteristics: If rhododendron are America's favorite evergreen shrubs, then lilacs are the favorite deciduous ones. They certainly are among the most nostalgic. Their fragrance brings back memories of courting on the porch swing or of stealing fragrant bunches of flowers from a neighbor's yard, and often, they remind one of Mom, perhaps because they bloom around Mother's Day in many parts of the country.

When we think of the lilacs, we picture the common lilac (*Syringa vulgaris*, Zones 3 to 7). These are the lilac-purple or white (*S. v. alba*) flowers born in terminal stems and filled with fragrance. But there are many others, including hundreds of hybrids of this plant alone (more than 400, actually). At one extreme is *S. v.* 'President Lincoln', one that is true blue, and 'Primrose', a creamy white that is too often listed in catalogs as "yellow." There are also many kinds with double flowers.

An unusual and very hardy lilac grows into a tree with glossy, waxy leaves. Japanese tree lilac (*S. reticulata*, Zones 3 to 7) makes an impressive landscape plant, especially in pairs flanking the walkway. It is very hardy (Zone 4) and grows to 30 feet. Late lilac (*S. villosa*) is even hardier, Zones 2 to 7. It blooms last of all the lilacs, into early summer. *S. patula* 'Miss Kim' (Zones 3 to 8) is a small shrub that is becoming more and more popular. It is sometimes called Korean or Manchurian lilac. Lilac-colored flowers become lighter as they fade.

The Persian lilac (*S. ×persica*, Zones 3 to 8) is a compact plant with fragrant flowers. *S. laciniata* has interesting lobed leaves that give rise to its common name "cut-leaf lilac" and to a different perfume. Hardy from Zones 4 to 8, it is one of the best lilacs to try for nostalgic northerners who relocate in Texas or Georgia. Meyer lilac (*S. Meyeri*, Zones 3 to 7) is known for its high flower-to-plant ratio. The flowers are violet and panicles shorter, about 4 inches long.

Cultural Information: Lilacs can grow in just about any garden soil—neutral to slightly acid is best; if it is too acidic, there may be no flowers. They should be fertilized every other year or so with a high phosphorus preparation—never an acidic shrub fertilizer. The plants will not bloom the first year after planting, but take a few years to settle in. Plants may have to be rejuvenated after several years. Go inside and remove the oldest wood and any spindly water sprouts or suckers that grow up straight from the base of the plant—up to one-third of the growth—at ground level. A cutback shrub will have fewer flowers the next year, but by the third year, will be producing more flowers than it did when it was in decline.

Flowers are produced on the last year's vigorous growth, so never prune until after or during flowering—you *must* cut these flowers and bring them in for the table and, especially, the nightstand. Dead-head if any seeds form, and don't feel guilty about cutting the neighbor's flowers all those years ago—it only led to more flowers the next year.

Syringa Meyeri

Tamarix ramosissima

Tamarix ramosissima

Tamarisk; see *Tamarix*

Tamarix ramosissima
(TAM-a-ricks rah-mo-SI-si-ma) **tam-arisk,** ESU. ○ –
Zones: 2 to 9
Height: 10 feet
Colors: Pink to lavender
Characteristics: This is a rarely seen shrub that is really easy to grow, and it can stand some pretty awful locations—for example, right by the seaside. Feathery, airy blossoms in warm pink are produced in early summer. The foliage is purple-green, and the growth is shaggy. Try to see this plant at a botanical garden or nursery. It might be for you, perhaps to grow at the rear of the sunny flower border.
Cultural Information: Well-drained, even sandy, soil is best. Prune in early spring.

Tartarian dogwood; see *Cornus*

Tree peony; see *Paeonia*

Trifoliate orange; see *Poncirus*

Viburnum (vy-BUR-num) many
Native Americans, SP, SU. ○ ◑
● ✿ –
Zones: Varies
Height: 4 to 15 feet by species and variety
Colors: White, pink
Characteristics: Vying for first place among the shrub genera for sheer scope and variety are the viburnums. Some are deciduous giants, others are evergreen dwarfs. All of them flower—mostly in umbels (flat flower clusters) of white or pinkish white sterile or fertile flowers.

Some have tubular flowers that end in stars, somewhat like those of the daphne. Often these types, such as Koreanspice viburnum (*Viburnum Carlesii*, Zones 4 to 7), are intensely fragrant. Others have flat umbels with sterile flowers surrounding fertile ones, like a lace-cap hydrangea, and those often lead to extremely ornamental fruits, such as the highbush cranberry (*V. trilobum*) and its European counterpart *V. Opulus* (Zones 3 to 8). These two have bright green, maplelike leaves and are deciduous. *V. Opulus* 'Sterile' is the snowball bush, which has only sterile flowers in perfect 2-inch to 3-inch balls, first green and then bright white. *V. plicatum tomentosum* is the double file viburnum whose flowers resemble a dogwood's showy bracts. Semievergreen leatherleaf viburnum (*V. rhytidophyllum*, Zones 5 to 8) is as well known for its leaves as for its flowers and fruit. They are long and puckered. These plants are related to the honeysuckles, a fact that can be recognized by the fruits. Many are beautiful and often in colors of orange or red. Some fruits are translucent and some persist until the following spring. Generally, these are tall shrubs for the landscape. They can be grouped into a collection or featured as specimens for almost any situation.

Cultural Information: These popular shrubs owe some of their fame to their ease of culture. They will accept various climates and soil conditions, but for the most part, they want a moist, slightly acidic medium. They also are not too picky about sunlight, and many varieties do well in partial shade, some in shade.

Prune away any dead wood after flowering. And watch out for water sprouts on some varieties— tall whips that shoot up from the soil level, or low on the trunk. These can be cut down at the ground or cut back to a place where other shoots branch. They too will branch and blend in. Also this will produce more branches on which flowers can develop.

Virginia sweet spire; see *Itea*

Viburnum opulus var. sterile

Viburnum sieboldii

Vitex Agnus-castus

Vitex Agnus-castus (VY-tex AN-yus-KAS-tus) **chaste tree, vitex,** SU. ○ ◑ ✿ –
Zones: 7 to 9
Height: 6 feet
Colors: Violet, blue
Characteristics: The chaste tree has fragrant lilac-blue flowers in summer for a very long period of time. The bark and leaves are fragrant too, when crushed or bruised or even brushed as you pass by. Not familiar to many gardeners, this is a long-cultivated plant.
Cultural Information: In many areas, the chaste tree can be treated like a buddleia, that is, it can be cut down to about 1 foot high in early spring. Don't be alarmed if the plant looks dead: Vitex rarely sprouts leaves before June, but by July, it is in flower. For this reason, it might be best to blend it with herbaceous perennials, or even roses, where its dormant twigs can be hidden from view. It is an excellent flowering shrub in its zone range.

Weigela florida (wy-GEE-la FLO-ri-da) **weigela,** ESU. ○ ◑ –
Zones: 5 to 8
Height: 8 feet
Colors: Red, pink, white
Characteristics: Sometimes, one wonders why so many people fuss about crab apple cultivars, or some esoteric shrub newcomer, when some of the tried-and-true, old-fashioned ones are just about perfect and bloom for such a long period. Weigela have trumpets of deep and light pink that completely cover the shrubs for more than a month from late spring to early summer. It creates a large fan shape that can get a bit out of hand, but can be pruned with impunity after the main burst of flowering ceases. There will be sporadic blooms throughout the summer.

Grow the weigela alone, with other shrubs or even at the back of the perennial border. Try growing a clematis up through the weigela, one that blooms in a complementary or harmonious shade at the same time, for a most wonderful effect. There are cultivars with white flowers or darker pink, and there is a variegated one that is not as vigorous as the species. *Weigela florida* 'Eva Supreme' is a dwarf with red flowers. *W. f.* 'Bristol Ruby' is also red flowered, but a giant, up to 10 feet tall.
Cultural Information: Plant it and forget it. This is terrifically

Weigela florida

easy in ordinary garden soil. Often, you'll inherit this plant along with a "new" old house. If it is woody and misshapen, it can be severely pruned to bring it back. Take out some of the old growth right at ground level and trim away any spindly, wispy branches. Feeding with a fertilizer high in phosphorus and top-dressing with well-rotted cow manure will be appreciated then. Sometimes long branches will touch the ground. Anchor the stems about 10 inches from the end with a rock, and next year, you'll be able to cut off a new plant to give to a friend or to plant in another part of the garden.

White forsythia; see ***Abeliophyllum***

Winter hazel; see ***Corylopsis***

Winter sweet; see ***Chimonanthus***

Witch hazel; see ***Hamamelis***

PESTS AND DISEASES

A drive through one of America's older communities quickly illustrates the inherent sturdiness of many of our flowering shrubs. Like the solid prewar homes they surround, the forsythia and lilac, weigela and *Kolkwitzia*, quince and spirea proved tough enough to stick around for the next generation of homeowners to enjoy, too.

Even many of the more finicky subjects can be grown without great difficulty in the home landscape, provided they are planted in the right site and given the care they require. As discussed in chapter 3, a disregard for a plant's basic needs and preferences is just plain wasteful and an invitation to disaster. The best policy of all is to plant the right plant in the right place. A true shade lover will be weakened by the rigors of full sun; a sun lover banished to life in a dark corner will never be vigorous. Diseases and pests will have their way with these weaklings first, and dispatch them most easily. When shopping for plants, look for disease-resistant strains like the new crape myrtles developed by Donald Egolf and introduced to the nursery trade by the U.S. National Arboretum, including 'Catawba', 'Powhatan' and 'Seminole'. Among the honeysuckles, for example, *Lonicera tatarica* 'Arnold Red' is more resistant to aphids than many others. Plant breeding programs worldwide will continue to place major focus on incorporating improved resistance into new varieties; ask your county Cooperative Extension for updated lists of such strains before shopping for new additions to the garden.

Recently, new interest in native species for plants has emerged, and a growing number of nurseries are propagating these old-timers. Proponents believe that natives are inclined to possess inherent tolerance to local climate conditions, having evolved along with the particular habitat. Natives also ask less in the way of water and fertilizer than many hybrids, so they are said to be more environmentally sound choices for the landscape.

Sometimes, even when a good-quality plant is planted in a proper site and well cared for, it does become sick. When this happens, there is no substitute for proper, and immediate, diagnosis. If a shrub is droopy, don't just water it automatically, assuming it's thirsty without checking other indications. The droopiness may be a result of *too much* water or of a bacterial wilt or other disease, such as a fungal canker or root rot. Don't jump to conclusions; ask for help in confirming your suspicions *before* you act.

Describe the symptoms of the affected plant to the horticulturist at your local nursery, botanical garden or Cooperative Extension; better yet, take a sample in to the Extension for evaluation and diagnosis, which is usually available at a small fee or no charge. Many outbreaks of pests and diseases are related to weather conditions. These local experts are in tune with what's out there and can help you pinpoint and solve your problem fast, minimizing guesswork that could otherwise prove costly or even fatal to the ailing shrub.

As with health problems in people, the end result of many plant problems can be moderated by preventative care and early diagnosis. Stay in touch with your garden by checking plants carefully each week, including the undersides of leaves and the bark of trunks and branches. Before a few aphids on the viburnum swell to a horde of sufficient force to overtake the whole garden, you can spray them away with a strong blast from the garden hose or an application of insecticidal soap and water. Likewise, it is better to cut out a portion of a forsythia's wood that is affected with nodular lumps called "galls" than to have the disease spread to the whole plant.

A KINDER, GENTLER APPROACH

Over the last decade, there has emerged an increasing awareness of the environmental impact of traditional agricultural methods. Too many of the chemicals touted as miracles in the postwar era proved to be poisonous. In response, federal and state agencies have put substantial money into developing large-scale pest-management strategies that rely less on chemicals for their effectiveness.

A new, still-emerging era of organic farming has been born from this research, but for the small-scale home gardener with a honeysuckle full of aphids or a rhododendron beset with borers, there were still many questions left unanswered. Were there alternatives to the traditional chemical controls for these problems? Fortunately, in the last several years, enterprising and environmentally concerned companies like Safer and Ringers have begun to introduce natural pest- and disease-control products geared specifically to home-garden use.

The staff at Burpee is encouraged that the healthy garden, healthy environment movement continues to build momentum. In the last year, the USDA's network of land-grant universities (the ones that administer each state's county-by-county system of Cooperative Extensions) have begun to recommend nonchemical methods to eradicate insects and disease,

whenever such an alternative is available, before advising gardeners to resort to traditional chemical controls. This least toxic approach is part of a system called Integrated Pest Management (see pages 82–83) that has already made great changes in the way the nation farms and gardens, and holds great promise for the future of the earth.

As simplistic as it may sound, good housekeeping is the cornerstone to maintaining a healthy garden. Although there are a few pests capable of traveling great distances, most begin and end their life cycle within a relatively small area, leaving the next generation poised to repeat the chain again. Often, they hide under debris such as fallen foliage, which is best carted away to decay in the compost pile, where it will become next year's natural fertilizer. Don't put parts of diseased plants in the pile, though; put them in the trash. Watering practices, if incorrect, can sometimes do more harm than good, inviting fungal pathogens like mildew, leaf spot and root rot to have a field day. Drip-irrigation systems, soaker hoses or other underground and on-the-ground watering devices eliminate the problem of wet leaves caused by overhead sprinkling.

Sometimes, shrubs are victims of other gardening practices, such as the way we care for our lawns. Bark injuries

inflicted by mowers and string trimmers can spell death for shrubs. Keep these hazards well clear of woody plants.

Besides being potentially harmful to the environment and ourselves, herbicides, fast-release fertilizers and other lawn-care chemicals are often too much for shrubs to handle. In what is like a slow death by poisoning, small doses administered on the nearby grassy areas season after season leach into the shrubs' root zones and finally become lethal. If you must fertilize the grass, switch to a slow-release formula of at last 50 percent organic ingredients. Instead of toxic herbicides, consider old-fashioned mechanical removal: Dig out the weeds.

On a similarly old-fashioned note, why not invite the birds back into your garden? By minimizing use of chemicals, installing even a small water source like a birdbath or small pool, providing nesting sites and some shrubby cover areas and planting berry- and seed-producing food sources, you will attract your own organic bug patrol. A few bedraggled leaves are no longer sufficient incentive for the use of chemicals. Gardeners who care about the environment must learn to tolerate some of these signs of nature at work and cease to try to interrupt and dominate the cycle.

Pollution-tolerant Flowering Shrubs

City gardeners are always looking for colorful additions to plain green yews, small Asian hollies and evergreen rhododendron. It's true that those shiny, green plants are good for urban gardens. Their leaves wash clean in every rain storm. But there are some of our flowering shrubs that have proved to be tolerant to one of the city backyard's worst problems, and also the problem of the urban and suburban front yard: pollution. Areas along the suburban roadway may be subjected to more pollution than many an urban backyard.

Amelanchier species (serviceberry, shadblow)

Camellia species (camellia)

Chaenomeles species (flowering quince)

Cornus alba 'Siberica' (red-twig dogwood)

Deutzia species (deutzia)

Forsythia species (forsythia)

Hydrangea species (hydrangea)

Hypericum species (St.-John's-wort)

Kerria japonica (Japanese kerria)

Mahonia Aquifolium species (Oregon holly grape)

Mahonia Bealei

Philadelphus species (mock orange)

Prunus species (flowering cherry, plum, etc.)

Rhododendron species (evergreen rhododendron)

Ribes species (flowering currant)

Spiraea ×*Bumalda* (spirea)

Viburnum species (viburnum)

Relatively Trouble-free Shrubs

Aronia arbutifolia (red chokeberry)

Aronia prunifolia (black chokeberry)

Calycanthus floridus (Carolina sweet shrub)

Caryopteris ×*clandonensis* (blue mist)

Ceanothus americanus (New Jersey tea)

Cephalanthus occidentalis (buttonbush)

Clethra alnifolia (sweet pepperbush)

Cornus mas (Cornelian cherry)

Corylopsis species (winter hazel)

Forsythia ×*intermedia* (Forsythia hybrids)

Forsythia species (Forsythia)

Hamamelis species (witch hazel)

Hydrangea paniculata 'Grandiflora' (peegee hydrangea)

Kolkwitzia amabilis (beautybush)

Lindera Benzoin (spicebush)

Lonicera species (bush honeysuckle)

Nandina domestica (heavenly bamboo)

Pieris floribunda (mountain andromeda)

Potentilla fruticosa (shrubby cinquefoil)

Prunus triloba (flowering almond)

Rhododendron maxima (rose bay rhododendron)

Spiraea ×*Vanhouttei* (bridal wreath)

Symphoricarpos species (snowberry)

Viburnum species (viburnum)

Leaves damaged by the following pests, from left: beetles, flea beetles, caterpillars, aphids, and leafhoppers.

Diseases

LEAF SPOT: A common fungal disease, particularly in wet or humid weather. Spots develop on leaves, which may eventually drop. Prune out diseased parts of plants. Allowing for good air circulation when planting can help minimize this problem. An organic fungicide may help check spread.

CROWN GALLS: Nodular growths near the soil line, caused by soil-borne bacteria, that can cause shrubs to weaken and die. Galls may be present on branches, too. Check nursery stock carefully. In the garden, remove infected plants and burn or discard in the trash.

FIRE BLIGHT: Bacterial disease that causes leaves to look as if they were exposed to fire. Remove diseased wood, disinfecting shears between cuts with rubbing alcohol.

POWDERY MILDEW: Powdery white buildup on leaves, especially of lilacs, common in humid weather or where air circulation is poor. More ugly than dangerous, but may damage flower buds. An organic fungicide may help prevent severe infestation.

ROOT ROT: Fungal or bacterial ailment encouraged by overwatering or excess rain, especially in areas of poor drainage. Dig out and destroy sick plants. Improve drainage by adding organic matter to the area. In the case of foundation-planted rhododendron that are yellowing, for instance, you should suspect a fungal root rot, common to these shrubs when incorrectly planted in the wet, hot alkaline soil of such spots.

RUST: Leaves and sometimes stems have rusty orange patches caused by a fungus. Leaves may drop. Good sanitation—removal of infected plant parts—is essential.

IPM: A Kinder, Gentler Way

Chemicals were hailed as miracles when they came into widespread use in the postwar years. Now many of these substances are better known as the unwitting culprits in the case of our failing environment, and each year more and more of them are going the way of DDT, banned from commercial or individual use. Not so far in the future, the garden center shelves will look less like a pharmacy.

Whereas once, and not so long ago, it was widely held as good cultural practice to treat lawns, shrubs and trees routinely to prevent outbreaks of pests and diseases, a new consciousness is spreading in the worlds of agriculture and gardening. It has been spawned by the advent of Integrated Pest Management

(IPM), a philosophy that employs a series of decision-making steps to arrive at the least toxic approch to each outbreak of trouble. IPM is not an organic approach, strictly speaking, because it does allow for the use of chemicals when, and only when, all else fails. But what has been demonstrated on farms, at land-grant universities doing IPM research and in botanical gardens (more and more of which have begun to try the principles of IPM the last few years) is that the application of chemicals can be reduced by 90 percent by following this approach, compared to the amount used with the old blanket-spray, prophylactic use.

IPM employs a combination of tactics to help gardeners make the

decision of how to cope with problems. The most important is monitoring: assessing the actual presence of pests instead of just assuming they're present, in a particular month on a particular plant—the old blanket-spray approach.

As it applies to growing ornamental plants like the flowering shrubs, IPM asks us to think about our aesthetic threshold of damage. Does the presence of a few chewed-up leaves warrant spraying a whole stand of "rhodies?" Can we learn to live with a little imperfection, with nature's way? Is the problem serious enough to warrant chemical intervention?

Before anyone practicing IPM resorts to chemicals, a number of safer alternatives must be exhausted. Can the

pests or diseases be eliminated mechanically—picked off, cut out or dislodged with a stiff spray from the garden hose? Can other cultural techniques such as pruning to improve air circulation, altered watering practices, quarantine of a sick plant or better garden sanitation eradicate the problem? Can the offending insects be trapped with the use of a pheremone (sex lure) or some other mechanical trap? Is a nontoxic spray such as one of the Safer brand products a possibility? Are there any predatory insects that can be called in to reduce the bad bug population or is there some other form of biological control, like a parasite or pathogen, that can be used? If spraying turns out to be the only answer,

Pests

APHIDS: Soft-bodied, pear-shaped insects that suck plant juices. Look for curled leaves, traces of secretion called "honeydew" or for licelike insects, particularly underneath leaves. Aphids probably won't kill a shrub, but can transmit viruses that can be dangerous or lethal.

A stiff spray of water from the hose or application of solution of insecticidal soap or horticultural oil will smother them.
BORERS AND MINERS: Difficult pests that can devastate shrubs by boring into wood (e.g., rhododendron borer) or mining between surfaces of leaves (such as in Tatarian dogwood). Among the hardest pests to control at

present without chemicals; remove infested plant parts and destroy.
WEEVILS: Insects that chew notches into leaves, especially in azaleas and other *Rhododendron*. Won't kill the plants unless infestation is allowed to go unchecked.
SCALES: Soft-bodied insects with hard shells, usually shiny

IPM suggests that it be done in a pinpoint manner, not a blanket spray at all, to focus simply on the affected plant part or parts. And IPM also recommends using the least toxic spray that will fit the bill.

IPM recommendations are being updated regularly as entomolgists continue to study the insect kingdom to devise ways to thwart costly outbreaks of pests. Meanwhile, though, the basic step-by-step strategy for arriving at the least toxic answer to each problem can be adopted by each and every gardener. Think before you act, it asks, especially when the subject is chemicals.

that they are a harmful species, because all of our butterflies and moths go through a caterpillar stage. Spray of a nontoxic biological control like Bt (*Bacillus thuringiensis*), a kind of "germ warfare" against caterpillars is very effective.

BEETLES: Leaf-eating insects. Handpick and kill Japanese beetles or use traps with scented lures placed away from the garden.

MITES: Like the tiniest of spiders, and often reddish in color, these creatures—not insects—congregate and suck on undersides of leaves. A strong spray of cold water may do the trick.

LEAF ROLLERS: These are the larvae of the common *Torticid* moth. The caterpillars cut leaves and roll them up, sometimes fastening them shut; and then they feed while protected inside the roll. They can defoliate entire shrubs.

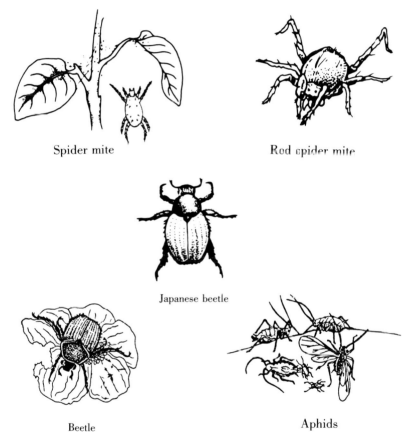

Spider mite

Red spider mite

Japanese beetle

Beetle

Aphids

and brown, sometimes white. These insects suck at sap of leaves and stems. Can be smothered with a coating of oil applied (sprayed) to plants when they are dormant. Read and follow all package directions.

CATERPILLARS: Perhaps the most familiar of all leaf-eating pests. Best to handpick most them, but only if you are certain

The ladies in Burpee's customer service department answering mail at the turn of the century.

GARDENERS' MOST-ASKED QUESTIONS

DESIGNING WITH SHRUBS

Q: Which shrubs are best for growing in a shady spot?
A: Glossy abelia (*Abelia × grandiflora*), azalea, hydrangea, witch hazel, some viburnum varieties, Carolina allspice (*Calycanthus floridus*), summer sweet, Japanese andromeda and mountain laurel.

Q: How can shrubs be used in a perennial border?
A: Shrubs can act as focal points in a flower border, providing height, winter interest and flowers. Choose shrubs in proportion to the bed, and place it/ them off-center for a more aesthetically pleasing, natural look.

Q: What flowering shrubs make good hedges?
A: Shrub roses, spirea, hydrangea, forsythia, bush honeysuckle, some viburnum and lilac.

Q: Which shrubs have the fewest pest and disease problems?
A: Native shrubs tend to have fewer pest and disease problems because they have adapted to the conditions in which they grow. Care must be taken, however, in selecting native species; choose shrubs appropriate to the kind of location where you intend to plant them. Rhododendron, viburnum, fothergilla, witch hazel, *Itea*, summer sweet, fringe tree, bayberry, dogwood, and many azaleas are especially satisfactory.

Q: Which shrubs bloom in summer?
A: Summer sweet, butterfly bush, some rhododendron, some viburnum and hydrangeas.

Q: Do any shrubs bloom in fall?
A: *Abelia × grandiflora, Camellia sasanqua, Hamamelis virginiana* and rose of Sharon all bloom in fall.

Q: Which shrubs are appropriate for growing in containers?

A: Some azalea varieties, camellias, *Pieris, Deutzia gracilis* and small spirea varieties.

Q: What kinds of shrubs work well for bonsai?
A: Azalea, forsythia and flowering quince all are charming.

Q: What kinds of shrubs work well espaliered?
A: *Forsythia × intermedia*, flowering quince and viburnum.

Q: What shrubs grow in acid soils?
A: Azalea, rhododendron, mountain laurel, *Pieris* and *Hydrangea*.

Q: What shrubs grow in wet locations?
A: Viburnum, summer sweet, sweet shrub and *Rhododendron viscosum*.

Q: What shrubs attract birds to the garden?
A: *Viburnum dentatum, Viburnum trilobum* and bush honeysuckle

are just a few. See page 21 for more suggestions.

Q: Which shrubs produce fragrant flowers?
A: Witch hazel, many viburnums, some azalea and rhododendron, summer sweet, lilac, rose, *Mahonia* and *Daphne*.

Q: Which shrubs have attractive berries?
A: *Viburnum dilitatum, Mahonia*, beauty-berry, fringe tree and snowberry produce exceptionally handsome berries.

Q: Which flowering shrubs work well as foundation plantings?
A: Try azalea, *Pieris*, deutzia, *Mahonia* and rhododendron.

PRUNING SHRUBS

Q: Can I prune shrubs to keep them the size I want?
A: Most shrubs can be pruned, but it is better to plant shrubs that will grow to the size you want rather than to keep pruning back those that naturally grow larger than you want them.

Q: Which shrubs are best pruned in spring, and which in summer? Does it make a difference?
A: Spring-blooming shrubs, forsythia and lilac for example, are best pruned right after they flower. They bloom on wood that grew the previous year and take all summer to form flower buds. Pruning at any other time would risk cutting off the flower buds. Summer-blooming shrubs such as rose of Sharon, for example, bloom on new growth and should be pruned in spring.

Q: Can hedges be pruned at any time?
A: Keeping the bloom times in mind, hedge plants can be pruned throughout the season.

Q: What is the best way to prune shrubs for a natural look?
A: Rather than shearing all the branches to the same height, for a more natural look prune back to an outward-facing bud or branch and remove the taller branches. Continue removing the taller branches until the hedge reaches the desired height.

Q: Is it important to prune shrubs?
A: Many shrubs, forsythia and butterfly bush among them, are rejuvenated when pruned yearly. Some benefit from being pruned every couple of years—lilac and azalea, for example. Some shrubs flower better when spent flower heads are removed; this is the case with rhododendron. It prevents seed formation and allows the shrub to use its strength for vegetative growth, and will benefit next year's flowering.

PESTS AND DISEASES

Q: How can I control Japanese beetles?
A: Japanese beetles can be a problem on many shrubs, especially crape myrtle and roses. They can be controlled in the long term by applying milky spore disease to the soil. Try to interest neighbors, too, in using milky spore. Milky spore takes a few years to become established, but will work for 20 years. It builds up in the soil over several years and paralyzes the digestive tracts of Japanese beetle grubs. The grubs die, never growing into beetles. Japanese beetle lures are also available, although they can actually attract beetles to your, or your neighbor's, garden. They can also be hand picked and dropped into a can of alcohol.

Q: How can I control scale?
A: Ladybugs attack scale in the crawler stage. Increase your ladybug population by ordering some to release in your garden from time to time. Safer's Soap is effective at this stage, too. Once scale attach to the branch, though, they are difficult to control. Dormant oil can be applied while the shrub is still dormant. Check with your Cooperative Extension agent to learn when the crawler stage occurs in your area.

Q: *How can I control powdery mildew? Do I have to?*
A: Powdery mildew commonly attacks lilacs during August's humid weather. There are few safe chemical treatments for powdery mildew. However, you can try sulfur-based sprays or dusts. The disease rarely kills plants, but it makes them unsightly and limits their ability to photosynthesize and make food. The disease is worse when plants are overcrowded and air circulation is poor. Keep your shrubs healthy and pruned for a more open shape and the problem should be lessened.

Q: *Will the powdery mildew on my lilac spread to my roses?*
A: No, powdery mildew diseases are host-specific. This means that the powdery mildew that attacks lilacs attacks lilacs only, and not roses. The powdery mildew that attacks roses can be more damaging to roses than the lilac disease is to lilacs, because it can destroy rose blossoms.

Q: *My azaleas are dying, but I can't see any insects. Could the problem be in the soil?*
A: Your plants may be affected by a soil disease known as phytophthora root rot disease. Unfortunately there aren't effective controls for this disease. If you think this may be the problem, have a soil sample tested for the pathogen by your Cooperative Extension Service. Remove any diseased plants and avoid planting related species in the same area. The disease can be more of a problem in poorly drained sites.

Q: *My rhododendron have comma-shaped holes on the sides of their leaves. What causes this?*
A: It sounds as though your rhododendron are being attacked by black vine weevils. These insects live in the soil and come out at night, so you may never see them. If you do see them, they will be identifiable by the long snout characteristic of weevils. The only controls are to spray the bugs when you see them with Safer's Soap, or use a chemical soil drench recommended by your Cooperative Extension Service.

GENERAL PROBLEMS

Q: *My fringe trees don't produce berries. What's wrong?*
A: Fringe trees and some other fruiting shrubs are dioecious, meaning there are male plants and female plants. Both sexes are necessary in the garden for fruit production. If you have healthy plants that produce flowers but neither berries nor fruit, your plants are probably the same sex.

Q: *I bought an azalea in full bloom last year, planted and watered it, and it grew well. It didn't bloom this year. What happened?*
A: Newly planted shrubs may not bloom for a year or more after transplanting because they spend their energy trying to get established in their new locations. Give them a couple of years and they will bloom if the location is favorable.

Q: *My hydrangeas aren't blooming. What's wrong?*
A: 'French Blue' or big-leaf hydrangeas are hardy in Zones 7 to 9 and flower buds are often killed in more northern areas. Not all blue hydrangeas are 'French Blue', and some varieties are hardier. Check to find out what variety your neighbors are growing if you live in an area cooler than Zone 7. Also, remember these varieties bloom on old wood and should be pruned after bloom. Remove two-year-old canes at or near ground level.

Q: *My lilac isn't blooming. What's wrong?*
A: When did you prune it? Lilacs bloom on old wood and so should be pruned after bloom. Young lilacs can take a few years to bloom, and old lilacs may become too overcrowded to bloom. Rejuvenate lilacs by removing the older stems every year or every couple of years. Sometimes breaking up the soil around the base of the plant encourages bloom because it stimulates root growth. Try working lime into the soil around the plant. Lilacs require six or more hours of sun.

Q: *My Exbury azaleas don't bloom. Why?*
A: Exbury azaleas prefer more sun than other azalea varieties and don't bloom well in shade. Prune them after they bloom, and avoid high-nitrogen fertilizers. They can take a couple of years to bloom after planting, as can most azaleas.

Q: *Why isn't my shrub honeysuckle fragrant?*
A: Not all honeysuckles are fragrant. Check that your variety was supposed to be fragrant. If so, it may be that your soil is lacking in certain trace elements. Have your soil tested for nutrient content and make sure the pH is within the range desirable for the plant.

Q: *Why haven't my butterfly bushes bloomed yet? I have had them for three years.*
A: Butterfly bush can take three years to bloom after planting, so yours is probably just on the verge. Don't prune in summer as this plant blooms on new wood.

Q: *My rhododendron are brown and dying back. What's wrong?*
A: This may be due to winter kill, especially if your rhododendron are in a sunny exposure in winter. Prune out dead areas, and consider moving the plants to a more protected location.

PLANTING

Q: *Is fall better than early spring for planting shrubs?*
A: As long as the plants are dormant, either season is fine. Fall planting is fine for many shrubs. It allows the shrub to develop some roots before the soil freezes, and gives it a headstart for spring growth. The next best time is in early spring, before the shrub breaks dormancy. Avoid planting shrubs when they have leafed-out, as it is more stressful for the plants to develop roots and foliage at the same time.

Q: *Which is preferable, bareroot planting or container planting?*
A: Bare-root planting allows the plant to establish a more vigorous root system in a well-prepared soil. Sometimes shrubs can become root-bound in containers, and it may cost them time and effort to adapt to your soil. Container-grown plants are easier to hold before planting; plant roots must be kept moist, and bare-root plants dry out more easily.

Q: *I just received my shrubs and they look dead. What should I do?*
A: Dormant plants can look very much like dead plants—just look at your garden in winter! Burpee tries to send dormant plants early enough for spring planting so that they can grow vigorous roots before they have to leaf-out. If you order late in spring, however, the rest of your garden may already be breaking dormancy. For fall planting, Burpee sends shrubs after they have gone dormant. The roots will continue to grow in the fall until the soil temperature drops to 40°F. Don't compare your established plants to the new dormant plants; they were kept in cold storage until shipping. Even in warmer weather, dormant plants may break dormancy slowly, as root establishment is a priority. Garden centers tend to sell container-grown shrubs that have broken dormancy, because they are seductively eye-catching. Mail-order companies send dormant plants because they ship better—as they can be shipped in cooler weather and can be sent at the best planting time. If you want to know if the shrubs are still alive, try scratching the newer growth with your fingernail. If the bark scrapes away easily to reveal fresh growth, you know your plant is still alive.

Q: *My neighbor's shrubs are already in bloom and mine are still dormant. Why are they so slow?*
A: Newly planted plants need to develop feeder roots before they can take up enough water and nutrients to support foliage and flowers. Be patient with newly planted plants! Your patience will be rewarded with healthier specimens.

Q: *I planted three shrubs at the same time. Two have broken* dormancy but not the other. *Is it dead?*

A: If you can see green on the stem when you scratch it with your fingernail, it isn't dead. Individual plants will break dormancy at their own rate. If conditions are good and the roots can grow, water your plants and be patient.

Q: *How can I hold my bare-root nursery stock until it is time to plant? It is still cold here and we don't plant until after Memorial Day.*

A: Bare-root nursery stock should be planted before the last frost. The Memorial Day planting date is usually taken to identify a time when all danger of frost is past, and is really later than you want to plant in most parts of the country. If you have to hold the plants for a week or two because you are unable to plant them, keep the roots moist and in a dark, cool location until you can plant. Check the roots every so often to make sure they are moist.

Q: *Do fall-planted shrubs require winter protection?*

A: If they are marginally hardy for your area it is a good idea to mulch the roots after the ground freezes. If you are planting a broad-leaf evergreen in a windy location, a screen can be constructed on the north and west sides by stapling burlap to wooden stakes driven into the ground. Or, you can spray an antidescecant, following the manufacturers' directions.

Q: *How should I prepare a planting hole for my newly ordered shrubs?*

A: Most shrubs arrive with planting instructions. However, in general, a hole is dug twice as deep and twice as wide as the root system; 18 x 18 inches is usually adequate. Mix organic matter such as peat moss with the soil before filling in the hole around the shrub's roots. See page 32.

Q: *Should I cut my shrubs back by one-third when I plant them?*

A: This is not necessary when planting container-grown shrubs. When you are transplanting shrubs from one part of your garden to another, on the other hand, you will lose some roots when you dig them up. (Bare-root shrubs probably lost some roots when they were dug as well.) To compensate for this loss, cut back some of the top growth (not more than one-third). This will make it easier for the plant's roots to supply water and food to the rest of the plant and enable the plant to become better established in the new location and more quickly.

MISCELLANEOUS

Q: *Why does it take so long for some young shrubs to bloom?*

A: Shrubs are longer lived than annuals and most perennials, and they take longer to mature. Some take longer than others; lilacs can take quite a long time. Plant annuals near your young shrubs to give your garden flowers until they are mature enough to bloom.

Q: *Is it better to buy larger rather than smaller shrubs?*

A: If you are willing to wait longer for flowers, it is generally better to plant smaller (but healthy) shrubs that can develop most of their root systems in your garden environment rather than that of the nursery. It is more difficult to transplant large shrubs than small shrubs, because more roots are lost in digging them up.

Q: *Can shrubs be grown from seed?*

A: Most shrubs, as is the case with most woody plants, are difficult for the home gardener to grow from seed. They can take more than a year to sprout, and they may require conditions for germination too complex for the home gardener to provide.

Woody plants are more slow growing than herbaceous plants. It is easier for most people to purchase shrubs that are several years old.

Please write or call for a free Burpee catalog:

W. Atlee Burpee & Company
300 Park Avenue
Warminster, PA 18974
215-674-9633

THE USDA PLANT HARDINESS MAP OF THE UNITED STATES

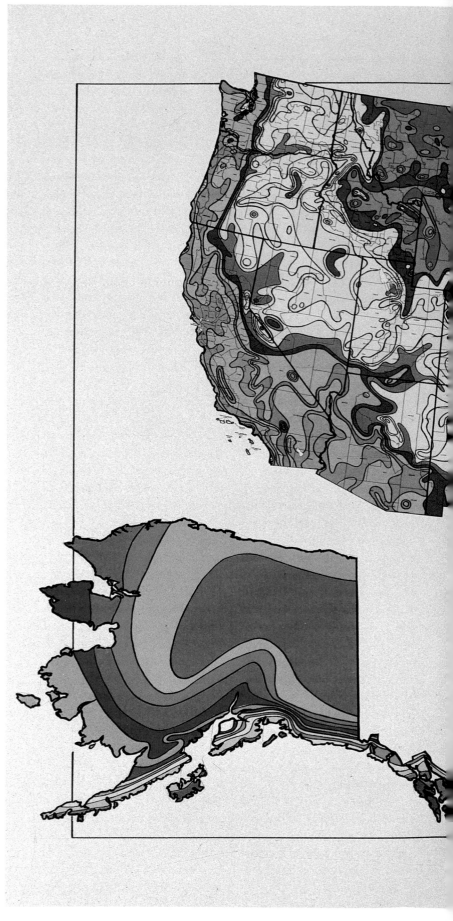

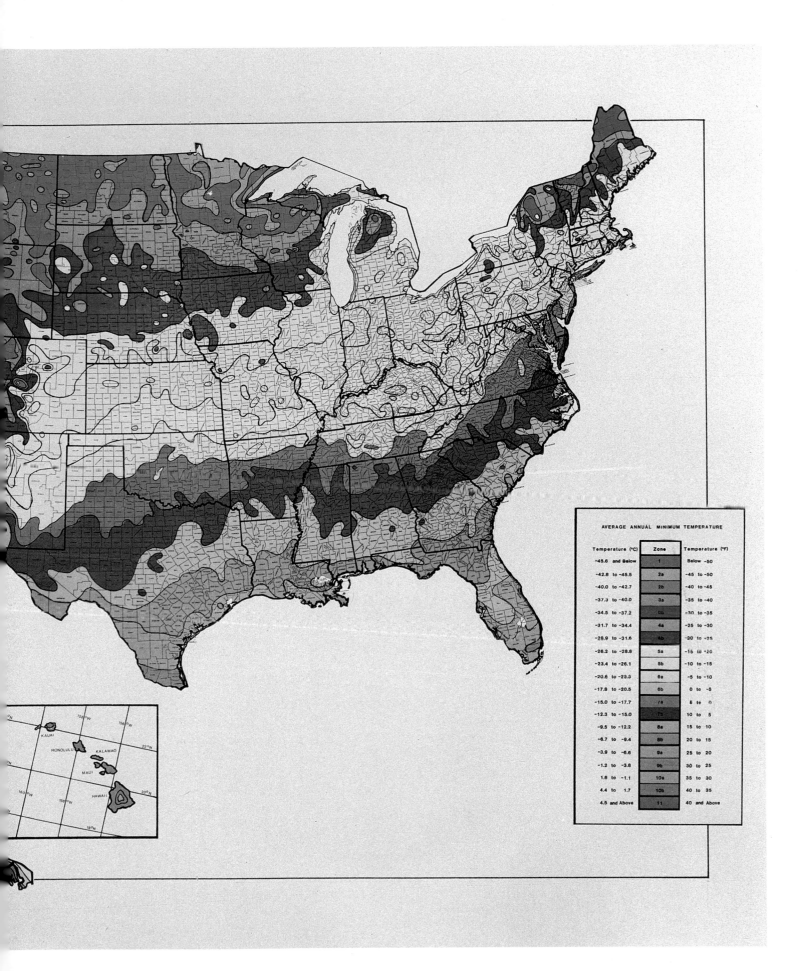

AVERAGE ANNUAL MINIMUM TEMPERATURE

Temperature (°C)	Zone	Temperature (°F)
-45.6 and Below	1	Below -50
-42.8 to -45.5	2a	-45 to -50
-40.0 to -42.7	2b	-40 to -45
-37.3 to -40.0	3a	-35 to -40
-34.5 to -37.2	3b	-30 to -35
-31.7 to -34.4	4a	-25 to -30
-28.9 to -31.6	4b	-20 to -25
-26.2 to -28.8	5a	-15 to -20
-23.4 to -26.1	5b	-10 to -15
-20.6 to -23.3	6a	-5 to -10
-17.8 to -20.5	6b	0 to -5
-15.0 to -17.7	7a	5 to 0
-12.3 to -15.0	7b	10 to 5
-9.5 to -12.2	8a	15 to 10
-6.7 to -9.4	8b	20 to 15
-3.9 to -6.6	9a	25 to 20
-1.2 to -3.8	9b	30 to 25
1.6 to -1.1	10a	35 to 30
4.4 to 1.7	10b	40 to 35
4.5 and Above	11	40 and Above

INDEX

(NOTE: Italicized page numbers refer to captions.)

I would like to thank many people who helped make this project a reality. First and foremost, Suzanne Bales, Margaret Roach and Victor Nelson, whose assistance in the preparation of this work was invaluable. Thanks also to my agent for this book, Helen Pratt. And to the staff at Burpee who have worked so hard for so many years to keep the company's high standards, especially Chela Kleiber.

Many gardeners provided inspiration as well as information, such as Helen Stoddard, Jean Pope, Steve Griffin, Pat Mason and landscape architects: Ray Thayer, Bill Wallis and the firm of Innocenti and Webel. I would also like to mention professional gardeners and the institutions that have helped so much: John Trexler of Tower Hill Botanic Garden; Marco Polo Stufano of Wave Hill Botanical Garden; The New York Botanical Garden and Brooklyn Botanic Garden.

At Simon & Schuster Anne Zeman, Rebecca Atwater and Rachel Simon.

And a special thanks to Ruth Levitan who has had a profound effect on my work since the moment we first met—many photographs of her magnificent garden appear in this book.

PHOTOGRAPHY CREDITS

Agricultural Research Service USDA
Bales, Suzanne Frutig
Cresson, Charles O.
Dirr, Michael A.
Druse, Ken

Drawings by Michael Gale (pages 35, 81 and 83) and
Frederick J. Latasa (page 34)